"Shannon's book is a witty, clear, and holy invitation to re-wild historical views of motherhood. Her words poignantly reimagine a God who is both divine and motherly. It is a must-read for those who desire a spiritual awakening in their calling of Christian motherhood."

—**Christy Bauman**, author of *Theology of the Womb*

"Evans takes us through the beauties, joys, depths, and pains of womanhood in this gorgeous and deeply personal reflection. *Rewilding Motherhood* is an invitation to take an inward journey into ourselves as women and mothers. Borrowing words out of her book, this is 'a permission slip that doubles as a ticket to a more awakened spiritual life.' With thoughtful, beautiful, and poetic prose, Evans points us toward a wilder, more liberative God, which in turn frees us to explore the divine feminine within us and the sacred mystery within our children."

—**Kat Armas**, host of *The Protagonistas* podcast; author of *Abuelita Faith*

"Evans's inclusive, communal perspective on motherhood is an invitation to shuck off cultural constraints and explore the women we've been all along. Weaving the sacred with the ordinary, Evans is our sister-guide for this journey of discovery. We are free to reconsider. Free to be mad. Free to embrace. Free to pray. Free to love from a place of wholeness. *Rewilding Motherhood* is the anthem we've long needed; this is a must-read for all who mother."

—**Shannan Martin**, author of *The Ministry of Ordinary Places* and *Falling Free*

"*Rewilding Motherhood* is the permission to explore what motherhood means outside of the traditional beliefs many of us believed were set in stone."

—**Tiffany Bluhm**, author of *Prey Tell: Why We Silence Women Who Tell the Truth and How Everyone Can Speak Up*

"Evans's prose leaves me breathless, like I'm standing above a rocky beach being buffeted by a storming ocean, soaking in the raw majesty and power. She shows her reader the cracks in our present reality, places where the Spirit breaks through. If you're feeling disconnected or disheartened by the waves of parenthood beating against the rocks of your soul, this book is for you."

—**Amanda Martinez Beck**, author of *Lovely: How I Learned to Embrace the Body God Gave Me*

"*Rewilding Motherhood* offers balm for mind, body, and soul, giving you permission to nourish your spiritual life as you care for your children. Gentle and strong, curious and encouraging, Shannon is a wise guide through the wild terrain of parenting's joys and struggles. Her words invite you to dig deeper, dream bigger, and search wider for the truths you have been seeking about God, your own life, and this sacred calling."

—**Laura Kelly Fanucci**, author of *Everyday Sacrament: The Messy Grace of Parenting*

"This soulful book is a strong, gentle embrace, welcoming us into an expansive exploration of the sacred spaces of motherhood. These reflections invite us to consider both our inner worlds and our larger communities, empowering all who possess a mothering spirit to have the unencumbered self-compassion to show up in our own hearts, minds, bodies, and souls, just as we show up for others."

—**Kayla Craig**, author of *To Light Their Way: A Collection of Prayers and Liturgies for Parents*; cofounder of *Upside Down Podcast*

Rewilding
Motherhood

Rewilding
Motherhood

Your Path to an Empowered
Feminine Spirituality

SHANNON K. EVANS

BrazosPress
a division of Baker Publishing Group
Grand Rapids, Michigan

© 2021 by Shannon K. Evans

Published by Brazos Press
a division of Baker Publishing Group
PO Box 6287, Grand Rapids, MI 49516-6287
www.brazospress.com

Printed in the United States of America

Library of Congress Cataloging-in-Publication Data
Names: Evans, Shannon K., 1983– author.
Title: Rewilding motherhood : your path to an empowered feminine spirituality / Shannon K. Evans.
Description: Grand Rapids, Michigan : Brazos Press, a division of Baker Publishing Group, 2021.
Identifiers: LCCN 2021009318 | ISBN 9781587435386 (paperback) | ISBN 9781587435423 (casebound) | ISBN 9781493432301 (ebook)
Subjects: LCSH: Mothers—Religious life. | Motherhood—Religious aspects—Christianity.
Classification: LCC BV4529.18 .E946 2021 | DDC 248.8/431—dc23
LC record available at https://lccn.loc.gov/2021009318

The author is represented by WordServe Literary Group, www.wordserveliterary.com.

21 22 23 24 25 26 27   7 6 5 4 3 2 1

For Irene, Nell, and Kay,
in honor of their motherhood

Contents

Part Two   Flowing Outward

Introduction

Not long ago I had a dream in which my neighbor, who is both a fiber artist and a mother of two, was pressing fabric into a basin of shallow water—ostensibly dying the fabric, perhaps, but I can't be sure. She was making art, one way or another, and she kept finding larger and larger containers to serve her purpose. Without frustration, without disappointment, she happily and with curiosity moved from vessel to vessel, seeking something vast enough to contain the wilds of her creativity.

When the basin failed to satisfy, she moved to a washtub; when the washtub did not suffice, she swapped it out for a kiddie pool; when the kiddie pool proved inadequate, she drained an Olympic-size pool in her front yard, stories and stories deep, astonishingly deep—we marveled together at how we hadn't known how fathomless the water had been all along. She covered the bottom with a shallow film of water and meticulously laid out the fabric inside, careful hands pressing out the creases. The result satisfied her, and she left the work to soak.

But a drained concrete pool of treacherous depths is not a safe thing to have sitting barrier-free in a little Midwestern neighborhood. In the dream I saw two of my own children heading over to play and I ran after them, knowing the danger they were in. The ground was covered with hornets that I stepped on as I rescued my little ones, muttering prayers of thanksgiving under my breath for their safety as I guided them home across the street, leaving my neighbor, her art, and a perilous cavern of imagination behind.

I awoke from this dream with pieces of it implanted in my bones. Weeks have since yawned by, but I cannot shake the knowledge that there was something archetypal at play in the image of my neighbor's labor. In dream language water represents the unconscious, and the act of exploring bigger and bigger containers for that inner world strikes me with incredible resonance—and not just for my own sake, but for the sake of mothers everywhere.

Because, if you think about it, this is what we do; we play at the edges of our unconscious, we explore the boundaries of our creative spirituality and suspect they go deeper than we can imagine. We long to give ourselves over to the mysteries of this inner life, and yet, we have responsibilities. We cannot neglect the physical and emotional needs of our children. We must be available to them, must protect them from all forms of danger. We can lose ourselves in the depths of our inner life, but only for so long before we must rein ourselves in once more. We make dinner. We do laundry. We tend to those in our care. We console ourselves that there will be a day when we can be baptized in the waters of Mystery, but today is not that day. Today we have children to dress and floors to sweep and eggs to scramble. The dream of the self that is spiritually alive—soulfully, creatively, holistically alive—is just that: a dream. We might touch it for a moment, but it is never ours to keep.

Few mothers I meet feel they are regularly in touch with that Mystery. Rather, most feel despondent about their spiritual lives, believing that somehow it is meant to be more than what it is but having no idea how to see that desire fulfilled. The path we took as younger women does not serve us now; there are no hours for silent prayer, no private moments to journal and weep, no time or energy for the community we used to have. So we put on a smile in the mornings, take our kids to worship on the weekends, flop exhausted on the couch in the evenings, and tell ourselves this might be all there is. And then we wonder why we can't feel content.

But contentment is not the apex of what we were made for. The feminine wisdom inside us knows this, and it is clawing to set us aflame in wonder and love. Let's face it, the deck has long been stacked against mothers thriving spiritually: our social, religious, and family structures together have forged a path that keeps us busy, preoccupied, self-denying, and obedient. These structures praise a woman who will give of herself but side-eye a woman who will belong to herself. The divine invitation is to be both women at the same time.

After all, we were women before we were mothers. But now there are days—maybe years—when we feel more like mothers than women, when the role of mothering subsumes the person we once knew ourself to be. Motherhood is an imposing figure in the room of the soul, and womanhood often bows in deference to her. But we are women, first and foremost. We were our own before we were ever anyone else's. And we have to find a way back to ourselves.

Not long ago I stumbled into reading about the ecological restoration practice of rewilding land, which heals damaged wilderness areas by removing all the harmful human intervention that has become so commonplace in resource management. To rewild a piece of land is to allow it to return to its original state: biodiverse and flourishing as nature intended. Rewilded land will look unkempt to the outside observer, but in actuality it is thriving—a fact proven by its self-regulatory and self-sustaining ecosystem.

When I read this something in me shifted, and I thought, *What if we could rewild motherhood?* What if, instead of confining women to some narrow social standard, motherhood could be the very thing to return us back to our original state as image bearers of an untamed God? If we removed all the harmful human intervention, could motherhood rewild itself into a healing and nourishing space in which to dwell? Dare I hope that if freed from the meddling of outside hands, my soul could be its own self-sustaining ecosystem?

Such rewilding is the intention of the book in your hands. It is not prescriptive, because there is no prescription for feminine spirituality. It offers few answers, because the questions you are asking are uniquely, perfectly, and frighteningly yours alone. But my hope is that it may serve as a nurturing hand to hold on your journey, leading you through the ins and outs of your ordinary life and inviting you to reimagine motherhood as the spiritually empowering experience it should be.

The Mystery within you cannot be confined to a basin or a washtub or a kiddie pool. The Mystery within you is miles deeper than you know, wondrous and treacherous and full of intrigue, beauty, and possibility. The narrow way forged for you by others is not the only choice you have. If you are ready to search the depths of yourself and trust what you find there, a wilder landscape awaits.

PART / ONE

Growing Inward

one

Forging Identity

Self-Actualization beyond the Roles We Serve

One of the greatest social myths of our day is that a woman can be totally fulfilled by motherhood. This is reiterated to us in many ways and through many voices: media, religious institutions, nostalgic family members (or sometimes, total strangers), perhaps our own lifelong yearning for children or battle with infertility. By the time we hold our first child in our arms, however they come to us, most of us have taken in the narrative hook, line, and sinker. *Behold, universe: I am a mother. I shall henceforth want for nothing.*

It's a compelling idea. The trouble is, I know no real woman who can honestly say this has matched her experience. I'm lucky to know many women who are incredible mothers and who are doing that mothering in incredibly different styles and circumstances. I have yet to meet one who desires nothing for herself beyond motherhood.

As someone who has wanted to be a mother since before I even menstruated, I can say that parenting my five children has exceeded my wildest dreams. My kids are incredible, but they did not arrive in tidy packages and suddenly deliver me from all personal desires and interests. My sons and daughter make my life more meaningful, but they do not exist to give my life meaning.

Mothers are fantastic at berating themselves for not being "content." This discontent, we are certain, is indicative of spiritual immaturity, or ungratefulness, or cultivating a bad, worldly attitude. But what if contentment is not the point? What if the idol of contentment actually holds us back from something greater? What if the idea of total contentment through motherhood is simply a bill of goods we've been sold?

Most mothers are not content; they are hungry—hungry for a deeper spiritual life, hungry for inner healing, hungry for intimate friendships, hungry for more of themselves. Yet we are immersed in a society that has always told us the hunger of women is bad. Dangerous. Undesirable. We have been indoctrinated in every possible way to believe that our hunger will make us too big, too indelicate, too uncomfortable to be around. *Here, have this small salad and be satisfied. Here, have this small life and be content.*

We long to follow that gnawing hunger, that instinctual knowing that tells us there is yet more transformation to lay hold of. But there never seems to be enough time for that sort of thing. After all, there are mouths to feed, appointments to keep, games to attend, baths to give. The work of her soul is never the most imminent need in a mother's line of vision. There is always something else to be done first.

That motherhood leaves a small margin for personal time is a reality no one would deny. But there is a greater reality available to us, one in which the spiritual vibrancy we seek is actually realized by examining more deeply *the very things we are already doing.* The limitations on a mother's time are real, but the rhythms of that burdened time can serve the life of our soul, not diminish it, and we will explore the ways this is so for most of this book.

We would be remiss, though, to believe that busyness is the only scapegoat for our lack of inner growth when in fact larger, even systemic, factors are at play. We exist within a cultural (often religious) ideology that exalts selflessness as the most laudable quality of a mother. But this should give us pause. Why do we believe the loss of self is a noble goal?

Self-giving is an incredible human gift and a virtue that we should all seek to cultivate, whether male or female, mother or not. There is no disputing that in every healthy relationship and system, mutual self-giving must be present. The problem arises when the expectation of self-giving falls predominately on one person; and when it comes to mothers, our social narrative assumes this as a given.

In religious spheres in particular, we are inundated with messages that glorify the sacrificial nature of motherhood, which further perpetuate ideals that would have women throw themselves on the altar of our marriages and children. The voices in these spheres are well-intentioned—at least, mostly—and sincerely want to honor the vital role that mothers play in the lives of their children. But we have to examine the narrative; we have to ask hard questions and recognize when we are allowing ourselves to accept messages that are downright harmful to the women they are meant to encourage. When the selflessness of motherhood above all else is exalted, value is indirectly assigned to each mother based on how small she can make herself. The result is not true self-giving but needless martyrdom.

I can't tell you how many Sunday homilies I have sat through that have bestowed grandiose praise on mothers for their self-lessness and yet have failed to mention the many other qualities that mothers demonstrate: qualities like strength, resiliency, tenacity, leadership, and problem-solving, to name just a few. This has been true within both Protestant and Catholic churches

I've attended. In fact, thinking back on the churches I've been a member of for any significant length of time, I can recall only one in which selflessness was not preached as the crowning jewel of motherhood. It was the one where the pastor was herself a mother.

A Symbol of Self-Sacrifice

Years ago, as I was preparing to give birth for the first time while parenting our three-year-old adopted son through a difficult season, I came across an ancient symbol of a pelican mother piercing her chest and letting the drops of blood fall into the mouths of her hungry chicks. The symbol predates Christianity but was assimilated into the Christian tradition because of the obvious association with the blood of Christ shed to give life to human beings.

At the time of my discovery I was in a painful stage of motherhood: physically painful in that I would be facing the most excruciating experience of my life—childbirth—in just weeks, and emotionally painful in that my preschooler was suffering in ways I did not know how to alleviate. I was vehemently protective of both of my children and utterly overwhelmed by what they were requiring of me.

The pelican stirred something deep within me. It seemed to dignify the sacrifices I was making and affirmed the vital role I was playing in the continuation of life. It also doubled as a metaphor for the Eucharist but with a rare feminine quality I found fascinating.

So like any good millennial, I found an Etsy shop that sold necklaces with the image and ordered one. The artist was phenomenal, and the colorful pendant of the feathered mother and her wanting chicks left light pressure on my chest for several months, including during the birth of my son Moses. And then suddenly, one day, it was gone. The bleeding mother pelican had been such a source of affirmation to me that I almost never took the necklace off. But one day, in a rare departure from my norm, I did. And I haven't seen it since.

For several years I bemoaned the loss of that necklace, sorely missing the physical reminder of my spiritual reality. I considered replacing it but never did. I considered getting it as a tattoo (because I'm a good millennial, remember?) but never did that either. My sentimentality slowly faded until it became only me turning to my husband about once a year and asking, "Remember that pelican necklace? I hate that I lost it."

Only now, years later, it occurs to me that maybe losing it was exactly what I was meant to do. A self-sacrificing pelican mother symbolized my reality in an important way for one season of my life; it gave me comfort and pride. But I don't believe I was meant to identify with the pelican forever. My family is not an ancient myth, and I am not an archetype. No one can bleed forever and hope to live.

When Self-Sacrifice Becomes Unhealthy Martyrdom

Dr. Christena Cleveland, a social psychologist and director of the Center for Justice and Renewal, writes prolifically on overturning what she calls "whitemalegod." To her, "whitemalegod" is the false understanding of the divine that we have collectively bought into—a false understanding that permeates not only our religious institutions but all of society, and it serves to create unhealthy relationships with one another, with God, and with ourselves. Cleveland writes, "'Self-sacrifice as the pathway to significance' is one of whitemalegod's most impressive deceptions. He's constantly demanding our self-sacrifice because what better way to keep people in bondage to white patriarchy's dehumanizing hierarchy than to teach them that the more they sacrifice on behalf of the whole, the more significant they will be."[1]

This disordered theology goes far beyond any one religious tradition, though some sink deeper into it than others. Such thinking has permeated our collective view of God. And most of us—women, especially—have internalized this sick twist on self-giving for much of our lives, hoping that the more of ourselves we sacrifice for the greater good, the more value we will have to God. Sacrificial love is a beautiful thing. When it is tipped out of balance, it can easily turn into a toxic trap.

If we believe, however subconsciously, that our worth is earned by our self-denial, we will never believe how deeply good God says we really are. We will spend our lives becoming less and less, hoping it earns us the approval of Someone up in heaven, when the whole time the God-Within-Us has been asking us to listen, to trust, and to know ourselves, because *this* is the interior pathway to heaven.

Rejecting Perpetual Daughterhood

It's convenient to find our identity in motherhood. I won't say it's easy, because there's not much about motherhood that is. But there is a certain usefulness to having a clearly defined identity assigned to us in one single moment. It allows us to bypass the hard work typically required in establishing a sense of being. It tempts us with the possibility of defining ourselves by those we are in relationship with, rather than by a self that we have actually worked hard to come to know.

And it *is* hard work. When you have spent your entire life believing messages about selflessness and the importance of assenting to outside authority, becoming a woman who knows her inner voice and trusts it as divine movement is a long, hard-fought battle. But it is not without rewards.

If you've spent any time sitting through a Psych 101 class, you are likely familiar with Maslow's hierarchy of needs. The famous theory of human need and motivation is illustrated in pyramid form: physiological needs are the base, followed by safety needs, belongingness and love needs, esteem needs, and finally, self-actualization at the top. It is in this highest space where humans are able to become their fullest selves, capable of realizing all their potential as directed by an inner compass rather than by external rewards.

In a just world, every human being could meet each level of Maslow's needs. As it is, even thinking about self-actualization is a luxury many cannot enjoy because they are struggling at the lower tiers of the pyramid. Women who have been socially marginalized have twice the work cut out for them in pursuit of self-actualization, having to overcome prejudice, generational injustice, poverty, and severe stress alongside the internal spiritual work the rest of us are undertaking. There is a discrepancy of privilege here that must be acknowledged. The amount of time and energy I have available to give to my own enlightenment journey does not reflect that of a second-generation Latina woman who is working three jobs to support her family.

However, this inequality does not nullify the importance of the endeavor. In fact, this is why it's so vital that those of us who *can* pursue self-actualization *do* pursue it. The more people there are living out their full potential through a vibrant and healthy inner life, the more passion, innovation, empathy, and creative solutions we will see, resulting in a more equitable world for all. We must work for a world in which every single one of us can flourish—and this usually means starting with our own interior work.

What most often keeps comfortable, white, middle-class women like me from self-actualization is the deception that we are already self-actualized. We assume that since we are relatively healthy, happy, well-liked people, there is nowhere further to go. We believe that our comfortable lives prove we have long been on the track of personal fulfillment, when instead we have more or less walked a road that was laid out in front of us since the day we were born. In ways that include but are not limited to motherhood, women (and white women in particular) are culturally conditioned to maintain the status quo. This might be painful to swallow—the truth often is—but it is critical for us to honestly and with curiosity ask ourselves how this has been true in our lives, rather than rush to write it off as unfounded gaslighting.

In her groundbreaking spiritual memoir, *The Dance of the Dissident Daughter*, author Sue Monk Kidd recalls a time early in the process of her own inner awakening when she was working in her garden and was suddenly bombarded by a strange new awareness: "*I am grown, with children of my own. But inside I am still a daughter.*" She continues on to explain, "A daughter is a woman who remains internally dependent, who does not shape her identity and direction as a woman but tends to accept the identity and direction projected onto her. She tends to become the image of a woman that the cultural father idealizes."[2]

We who like to think of ourselves as modern, enlightened, independent women may balk at this characterization of daughterhood. But when we start peeling back the layers, we might be shocked by the approval-seeking conformity that we find deep within. Being a daughter gives us a place, gives us respect, gives us belonging and assigned value. But being a daughter can never give us back ourselves.

Shedding the Old to Find the New

When I found out I was pregnant for the first time, I immediately knew where I wanted to have the baby. Near the downtown area in our city, off a charming side road, was a small historic home with a large sign in the front yard that read "Inanna Birth & Women's Care" with a list of the names of several midwives under it. On the day of our first appointment, while our three-year-old Ugandan-born son, Alyosha, played nearby, a midwife sat across from us, smiling as Eric held my hand supportively, and said, "Let me tell you the story of Inanna."

Not seeing what this had to do with my pregnancy or future delivery, I humored her and let her continue. She proceeded to tell of the ancient myth *The Descent of Inanna*, considered by some to be the first epic poem ever written at around four thousand years old—even older than *The Epic of Gilgamesh*. In the story, Inanna descends to the underworld to visit her sister Ereshkigal, the queen of the dead, whose husband has just died. Naturally the underworld is not a safe place to go, so Inanna is armed with divine powers to protect her: a crown, two necklaces, breastplate, ring, scepter, and fine clothes. When she arrives, her sister Ereshkigal is none too pleased and orders the seven gates of the underworld bolted shut against Inanna. She is allowed through one gate at a time but is required to strip herself of one divine power at each gate, so when Inanna finally meets her sister she is naked and utterly vulnerable.

Ereshkigal turns her defenseless sister into a corpse and hangs her on a hook, where Inanna stays for three days and three nights, until her faithful servant Ninshubur goes to the underworld with two demons, outsmarts Ereshkigal, and revives Inanna with the food and water of life. Inanna then rises from the dead and returns to earth.

When the midwife finished the story, she looked me in the eye with all the tenderness of a wizened sage who knows their protégé cannot yet possibly understand what they are about to say. "This is childbirth. You will be stripped of everything, for you can take nothing with you but what is inside you. You will die and you will be resurrected. You will know true things about yourself for the first time. And if you are paying attention, you can take that knowing with you into the rest of your life."

This is the sacred mystery of motherhood, whether it has been entered into through childbirth, adoption, foster care, step-parenting, or any other way. Motherhood does not tell us who we are; motherhood tells us how to find out for ourselves.

—— Going Deeper ——

Find a comfortable place to sit with a journal and a pen. Set a timer for ten minutes and write down everything that comes to mind about identity and motherhood. No one will ever see this, and there are no right or wrong answers. Just let your mind free-associate as it will. When the timer goes off, look back on what you've written and ask yourself the following questions, or any other questions that seem important for your inner process:

In what ways have I hidden behind motherhood as my identity?

When I think about separating my role as mother from my identity as a person, what fears do I experience? What hopes?

What is something I have always wanted to do or learn about but have not pursued because it felt silly, selfish, or otherwise out of line? Could there be a divine invitation for me there?

What messages have I heard about God requiring my self-lessness? Does that feel true in the deepest parts of my being?

When you are done, sit in silence for a few minutes. Then breathe this prayer:

I do not have to become small for you to value me. You invite me to take up space.

two

Maintaining Boundaries

Generosity toward Self and Others

We are irrevocably, unapologetically changed by our children. Author and activist Glennon Doyle has said that her firstborn "brought me into this world," because finding out about the pregnancy ushered her out of addiction and into sobriety.[1] Doyle's circumstances may be unusual, but her words resonate with many of us who sense we have been birthed into the world in a new and deeper way by the arrival of our children. Once they come into existence we are never, ever the same.

This truth that mothers have known in our bones for centuries has been evidenced scientifically in our lifetime. The medical community now recognizes that cells from the baby cross the placenta and enter the mother's bloodstream, eventually becoming part of her tissue. If you are a mother who carried your child in your womb, pieces of their DNA are still inside of you—and always will be.

That is one hell of a bond.

It's mysterious. It's magical. The connection between a mother and her child is both physical and metaphysical. This is the holiness of our motherhood. Yet this can also be our demise, because how can a woman extricate herself from an interlacing of being that runs so deep? We literally have pieces of our children inside of us—how can we be expected to continue on into a life separate from them?

In her best-selling novel *Little Fires Everywhere*, author Celeste Ng crafts one of the most potent descriptions of the ache of motherhood I have ever read. Of children growing up, Ng writes, "Parents learned to survive touching their children less and less. . . . The occasional embrace, a head leaned for just a moment on your shoulder, when what you really wanted more than anything was to press them to you and hold them so tight you fused together and could never be taken apart. It was like training yourself to live on the smell of an apple alone, when what you really wanted was to devour it, to sink your teeth into it and consume it, seeds, core, and all."[2] To someone who is not a parent, Ng's words might sound extreme—bizarre even. But motherhood has a way of making you a bit odd.

And yet we know we can't devour the apple. Apples need to be free to be their own little appley selves. We know that clinging too tightly to our children does not benefit them in the long run; we assent fairly readily to that fact, even when living it out is much harder. But do we understand that we too are damaged when we become indiscriminately intertwined with our children? Can we see that it is not only they, but also we, who cannot grow strong and able if our roots are gnarled around another living thing?

Preserving our emotional, mental, and physical health as mothers requires that we institute clear boundaries about how much self-giving we offer. This does not mean holding our children or partners at a distance—far from it. Part of the sacredness of womanhood is our fundamental gift of relationship:

we nurture, we include, we embrace. We are warm, soft, safe ports for the tiny ships of our children to return to after a daring adventure. We were made to be in deep relationships with our loved ones, and when we do it well, we thrive. But when we don't do it well, we suffer all the more.

Boundaries come in both external and internal forms, and we all need some combination of both to be our best, most whole selves. *External boundaries* serve our interpersonal relationships, helping us identify the treatment we will and will not accept from other people, as well as helping us differentiate our individual selves as separate from the people we care about.

Here are some examples of external boundaries that have been set by mothers I personally know (names and some details have been changed to protect their privacy):

- Natalie determined that because of health issues she could not handle having more than two kids, even though her partner strongly desired more. She was the primary caregiver, and limiting her family size was crucial for her well-being.

- Amy was laid off from her job but knew that working outside the home was something that kept her healthy, even if it was not financially necessary for her family. Despite pressure by some to become a stay-at-home mom, she kept her kids in daycare for months while she filled out applications and went on interviews—ultimately finding a new job that excited her.

- Selena enjoyed being the primary caregiver for her young children but recognized a need for a break by the time dinner came around every night, so she discussed this with her spouse. Now, every day after the meal is eaten as a family, she retreats alone while he oversees bath and pajama time.

- Katie used to find herself sucked into the rabbit hole of her spouse's cyclical bouts of depression, staying up late into the night talking with him and then feeling depleted the next day. Eventually she learned to communicate exactly what time she would need to stop talking and go to bed—and was pleasantly surprised to see her marriage improved by the change.
- Shanel had a challenging relationship with her parents but still wanted them to be a part of her child's life. She decided to continue making visits a few times a year but limited them to no longer than two days at a time.

Internal boundaries, on the other hand, are those that are self-imposed for our own welfare. When set and implemented well, internal boundaries enable us to treat ourselves with respect and make choices that move us toward inner wholeness.

Here are some examples of internal boundaries that have been set by mothers I personally know:

- Erin succumbed to alcohol abuse in the past, but these days she is in a healthier mental and emotional place. Moving forward, she has determined that no alcohol whatsoever is the right choice for her life.
- Swami does not own a scale because she has decided to assess her body's needs by the way it feels rather than the way it looks.
- Christi is active on social media in both personal and professional capacities but realizes that too much screen time can be unhealthy. Every six weeks she logs off all social media accounts for an entire week.
- Monique closes each day by recalling the events that unfolded and her responses to them, whether she is proud

of those responses or not. She then makes a mental exercise of separating her being from her behavior by noticing her mistakes and resolving to do better, while also affirming herself as a good and valuable person regardless of those mistakes.

Boundaries can vary from mildly consequential to life changing. Our lives are filled with both kinds, plus those that fall everywhere on the spectrum in between. Often we set boundaries without realizing we are doing it. But then there are other times when standing up for our needs feels like the hardest thing we've ever done. In those moments, setting boundaries can be an act of courage. In a very real sense, setting boundaries is a spiritual exercise in inner freedom.

Reclaiming Virginity

It has been a long time since I considered myself a virgin. I realize that as the mother of enough kids to form my own basketball team, this news will surprise no one. What might come as a surprise, however, is that I'm starting to reclaim the concept itself. The more I learn about the history of the word, the more I realize that although my hymen is no longer intact, I am living out virginity more truly than ever.

Kim Hudson, author of *The Virgin's Promise*, says the original definition of virgin was "to know your intrinsic worth."[3] Feminist philosopher Marilyn Frye says a virgin is a wild and willful independent human as opposed to subjugated property.[4] In Greek mythology, a virgin goddess is one who is self-fulfilling and makes her own choices. I have read in various places that a working definition of a virgin is a woman "who belongs to herself."

However we define it, there seems to be substantial evidence that virginity has not always been synonymous with a lack of experience of penetrative sex, which is what we generally mean when we use the word now. Understood in this broader context, it's fair to say that *virgin* could be a word for a person who has done her inner work to stay true to herself, her own needs, and her own voice, rather than conform to the demands or expectations of those around her—whether they come from individuals or society. It's actually quite handy to have such a word, especially in the conversation surrounding boundaries.

Kim Hudson developed her own theories about the significance of the archetype of virgin while studying the work of psychoanalyst Carl Jung. Hudson was enthralled by Jung's analysis of the hero's journey and the archetype of hero, but she perceived the absence of the feminine, a curiosity that eventually led her to discover the virgin archetype. It's important to note here that both men and women have elements of hero and virgin in themselves and in their stories; the archetypes are not gender exclusive but representative of the masculine and feminine elements that are present within all humans. Yet in the discussion of seeking spiritual wholeness in motherhood, the journey of the virgin carries much more weight.

Hudson describes the virgin's journey as a "creative, spiritual, and sexual awakening that creates a boundary between who we are and who everyone wants us to be."[5] While the archetypal hero must embark out into the world to find their true self, the archetypal virgin does so in the domestic realm. Sound familiar? Whether we work outside the home or exclusively within the home is not the issue; rather, all mothers by nature of our motherhood are tasked with finding meaning, identity, and spirituality right where we are. The boundaries of self must be created internally; we discover that we are a world all our own. While the task of the hero is to go out and become self-giving, the task of the virgin is to go inward and become self-fulfilling. "Whenever someone stands up for themselves, the virgin archetype comes out," says Hudson.[6]

Breaking Unhelpful Bonds

By the time I had my daughter Thea, I had already birthed and breastfed three babies in less than six years. She was the fourth. You can imagine how depleted and exhausted my body was by that point, and one day while breastfeeding I found myself mentally calculating the number of months left that I would have to use my body to feed a baby. We had already decided Thea would be our last child; I could almost taste the freedom that would come from sleeping through the night and not being relied on to produce food from my physical person. I had breastfed all of my biological babies for at least a year each, and I had found it to be a wonderful experience. The problem was, it no longer felt that way.

Oh, it did in the beginning, when she might as well have been a blind baby bird holding her mouth open for worms, but after months stacked on months, I'd become restless. The collective needs of my children were high, and breastfeeding began to represent something much heavier than just feeding a baby; it began to feel like a tangible ball and chain keeping my body from belonging to just me again. The fact that I identified with this metaphor troubled me. I'd known the feeling of empowerment that can come from breastfeeding a baby, and this wasn't it.

But with Thea being the only girl, I struggled with the possibility of her getting the short end of the stick: I knew breastfeeding was good for attachment and for nutrition. And regarding the latter, well, she was already such a little peanut, hovering at around the tenth percentile and eliciting "hmms" from the doctor reading her chart at each well-child visit. At the six-month checkup the pediatrician told me I would need to bring Thea back one month later to check her growth. Although I wasn't worried per se, it didn't escape my thoughts either.

I had always taken it for granted that I would breastfeed all my babies until they turned one; after all, I had no medical reason not to. I didn't want to deny Thea the quality of care I had given her brothers—especially knowing that as a female, she would likely have fewer advantages in other ways than my boys would have.

As I continued to do my own inner work through prayer, counseling, and seeking spiritual direction, I began to recognize my lifelong pattern of giving my body in service of others at the expense of self—a pattern that had created damaging relationships in my life and one I was determined to stop. I realized that weaning my baby would be an act of self-care, a way to put a stake in the ground and declare that I am entitled to set specific and tangible boundaries for my own wellness.

Yes, there had been a time when breastfeeding empowered me to become more of the mother I wanted to be. But this was a different time. This time breastfeeding my baby was actually making me less of the mother I wanted to be, one who was "touched out," resentful, and short-tempered. In an act of self-compassion, I weaned Thea onto formula at seven months old. Immediately, I felt psychologically healthier. I was kinder to my other kids. Suddenly my toddler's terrorist antics seemed more charming than enraging. Almost overnight, I began to enjoy motherhood again.

One month later we went to the doctor for Thea's growth check, and my eyes bulged at the number on the scale. She had gained two pounds in one month. The very thing that I'd needed to grow, she had needed too.

Boundaries Help Us Thrive

Setting boundaries can sometimes feel selfish. Many of us, especially in our roles as mothers or spouses, are slow to identify or implement the boundaries that would allow us to flourish because we feel guilty about the very idea of guarding our own needs so vehemently. Instead we run ourselves ragged trying to be what everyone else in the family is asking us to be, and the result is that we become resentful of the very people we love the most. There is nothing healthy or sustainable about such a system. It benefits no one.

The most surprising thing about setting and maintaining boundaries is that, rather than producing selfishness, it actually produces within us a greater capacity for generosity. This might seem counterintuitive, but think about it for a moment. Those who cannot set boundaries do not have the space in their lives to care for themselves in a way that allows them to operate from their healthiest state because there is always someone else to put first. So while it might look like these people are the most unselfish, helpful, and merciful people we know, the reality may be that deep down they feel trapped, resentful, angry, and overlooked.

On the other hand, people who have put in the work of implementing strong personal boundaries have created space in their lives for generosity. They are not wasting away inside, having spread themselves too thin to do anything wholeheartedly. They are able to give generously to others in ways that perpetuate cycles of life, energy, and joy.

"Generosity can't exist without boundaries," says author and University of Houston professor Brené Brown.[7] In fact, her data indicate that the most compassionate people she has interviewed are also the ones with the strongest boundaries. The working definition of a boundary that Brown uses is simple: it's the line between what's okay and what's not okay. In other words, research is telling us that to become more compassionate (read: spiritually healthy) individuals, we need to clarify with ourselves and with others what we are and are not willing to accept in life.

It sounds straightforward enough, but for us to identify and stand beside our personal boundaries, we have to first know what our needs are—and some of us moms haven't thought about our own needs in years. To know what boundaries would help us grow and thrive, we have to make space in our lives to stop and listen to the Spirit within: space to dull the noise, space to halt the hustle, space to be with ourselves in silence.

The first thing many of us will need, then, is to establish some boundaries around our time. This might look like making an arrangement with our parenting partner or a babysitter or another mom friend with whom we can arrange a childcare exchange. Getting time alone often feels impossible for mothers, but it is rarely impossible in actuality. It's a matter of prioritizing our own inner life, of deeming ourselves worthy to be a priority. If we can protect our inner life by giving it time to take root and sprout, we will find that the rest of our needs may finally have a place to make themselves heard.

—— Going Deeper ——

Settle into a seated position with your feet flat on the floor as an act of grounding yourself. Turn your palms upward as a gesture of receptivity to the wisdom and insight God wants to offer you. Take a few long, deep breaths and find stillness.

Allow yourself to reflect on your daily life from the time you wake up to the time you go to bed. Go through a typical day in chronological order, being sure to include people you interact with (children, spouse, mom friends, coworkers, boss, etc.) as well as things you do (household labor, parenting, work, etc.). As you reflect on the minutiae of your life, begin to notice where feelings of resentment arise. Where do feelings of envy emerge? What about feelings of longing? Remember that feelings are neither good nor bad; they are merely giving you information.

In a spirit of compassionate curiosity, ask yourself questions about the areas that elicited these feelings. Often strong internal movements like resentment, envy, and longing can be helpful indicators of an area in need of boundaries, whether internal or external. Allow yourself to dream about putting healthy boundaries in those places. What might they be? How would they feel? How might such a change create more generosity in your life, both toward others and yourself?

three

Holding Tension

The Sacred Work of Integration

Motherhood is fraught with tension. Every stage tantalizes our longing for clear-cut answers, for solutions as reliable as math equations, for outcomes and children to be predictable. The pressure to make the right choices is visceral, with arguably high-stakes consequences. Yet when we talk about the tensions mothers are asked to hold, we are not talking only about parenting decisions. We are not even *mostly* talking about parenting decisions.

On a spiritual plane, the brunt of the work before us is holding the tension between seemingly opposing forces in our own selves: the tension between desires, the tension between obligations, the tension between self-sacrifice and self-assertion. The tension between the person you are and the person you thought you'd be by now. These are the tensions that strike far deeper than our identity as parents; they strike down into the essence of our womanhood—down so far we might not even know they are there.

It's difficult to look these things square in the eye. It's much easier to give our attention to marital conflicts or child-rearing choices, those tangible pillars that our true self wants to hide behind. But identifying and reckoning with the nuanced places of tension is where the majority of our inner work lies. This is the foundation on which interpersonal work is built; it is not secondary to it, and if we neglect it our unhealth will rear its head in all sorts of ugly ways with our partners and children.

- Our work is to hold the tension between desires: the desire for autonomy and the desire to be available for our children, the desire for career opportunities and the desire for an ordered home, the desire for spiritual abundance and the desire for plain old comfort.
- Our work is to hold the tension between obligations: the obligation to children and the obligation to the adult world, the obligation to marriage partners and the obligation to our individuation, the obligation to household chores and the obligation to paid employment.
- Our work is to hold the tension between self-sacrifice and self-assertion: to expend ourselves for others without losing ourselves in the process, to live humbly and sacrificially without failing to advocate for our own worthy needs, to give of ourselves and belong to ourselves at the same time.
- Our work is to hold the tension between the person we are and the person we always thought we would be: to accept our failures as teachers rather than indictments; to assess our flaws and vices seriously, but with self-compassion; to reconcile the fact that we are more than who we are on our worst day, yet without hiding or dismissing that person either.

Feeling the Strain

The first time I realized I have a chronic inability to hold tension, I was in a yoga class two months after giving birth to my middle son, Taavi. The flaps of my postpartum body were still a foreign landscape. My wrecked abdominal muscles were still separated by several inches. Even though it wasn't my first rodeo, I was daily taken aback by the weakness and strangeness of the body I'd once known so well.

But I felt I owed this body something; after all, it had brought a pretty incredible human into the world and was now single-handedly producing food to keep him alive. I had enrolled in the yoga class on a bit of a whim, a small grasp at the self-care I knew I needed but didn't know how to describe, much less manifest. I've always been naturally flexible and slow moving, so yoga made sense as that rare form of exercise that didn't feel to me like Dante's ninth circle of hell.

The instructor was conducting a thoughtful and integrative class, and I was enjoying it immensely. Then she instructed us to enter the dreaded Lizard pose (*Utthan Pristhasana*, if you're Sanskrit-savvy), and suddenly it seemed like, shouldn't we maybe be wrapping up class now? *Gosh darn we're all out of time. See you guys Tuesday!*

As much as I wanted to head out for a strategically timed bathroom break, I reluctantly moved my body into the pose instead: one flexed foot at the top of the mat with a knee bent to the side, the other leg stretched out long behind, forearms resting on the ground. Many yoga poses are uncomfortable if you're doing them right; Lizard pose makes me want to jump out of my own nonreptilian skin.

We held the position for months. (I firmly maintain this.) Time dragged by, and I fantasized about folding my protesting limbs into the fetal position. But just as I neared the point of follow-through, the instructor's voice rang clear in the bare room: "Don't resist the tension; welcome it. If you can hold the tension in your yoga practice, you will train your brain to hold tension in your daily life as well."

People often speak of divine revelation as a door that is suddenly opened or as a lightbulb turning on. This moment was exactly that for me; the message buzzed like the sing of an arrow to the bull's-eye of my heart. It was holy.

I realized—and even now years later continue to be made aware—that throughout my life I have experienced one of two responses to feelings of tension: escape or resistance. There has been very little curiosity, very little integration. If I feel something that creates unrest or discomfort, my knee-jerk reaction has always been to make it stop as quickly as possible.

This happens in ways both obvious and subtle. If Eric and I are arguing, my natural responses have always been to either leave the room (go to bed, take a shower, etc.) or to become irrational and volatile, no holds barred. It is only with a lot of intentionality over the years that I have begun to work on staying calm and present in order to engage in the disagreement in a more healthy way.

A less conspicuous example might be my tendency to self-indulge as an escape. I don't care to report how many times I have found myself shopping the dollar bins of Target rather than untangling the complicated web of emotions I felt toward my children that day, but there are hundreds of other ways we escape our inner tension too. Scroll social media. Pour a drink. Stream a Netflix show. None of these are evil in and of themselves, but when they prevent us from doing the work of integration, the consequences to our souls may be dire.

Resisting the Urge to Walk Away

Five kids in, I'm still learning how to resist avoiding tension. I'm still noticing within myself the overwhelming urge to mentally, emotionally, and spiritually escape the uncomfortable parts of motherhood. I'm still having to run my own interventions. Sometimes, when I'm lucky, God runs them for me.

One such time occurred when Thea was a newborn. On this particular night, Eric was getting our four boys to bed on his own, and I was downstairs in the living room pacing with the baby across the room and back, over and over again. Finally, I stood still before the fireplace and let myself feel every ache that my body was calling to my attention: neck, shoulders, and back, all shouting for reprieve.

Thea had gastroesophageal reflux disease, and at our last appointment the pediatrician had advised holding her upright for at least twenty minutes after each feeding. This, supposedly, would keep my breast milk from shooting back up her esophagus like a dragon belching fire. Sometimes it worked, sometimes it didn't seem to matter. I had to make my peace with the flip of the coin.

All was quiet but the hiss of the fire, licking yellow against brick. It had been ten minutes since she'd nursed. Ten out of twenty. I sighed and reconvened my pacing when suddenly it hit me: an unignorable, indisputable desire to abandon ship. *Screw this.*

I was tired, bored, and itching to commence my nightly snack-eating and Colbert-watching ritual. An instinctual urge to escape filled my being—no matter that I knew the reflux would make me pay for it later. And right there, as clear as day, I felt the Spirit within me speak, just as it had that day in the yoga class years before.

"Stay."

Stay for ten more minutes. Don't run. Learn integration in places of discomfort. Learn to hold the tension between how you wish things were and the reality of how they are.

It was an invitation to mindfully practice strengthening a weak muscle. Was I free to put my daughter down for a while? Of course I was. But the moment represented far more than simply the choice of what to do with a spitty baby; it represented my ongoing interior battle with escapism. Do I stay present and available when I feel discomfort rising, or do I walk away from the opportunity for growth?

Acknowledging Hardship

In January of 2020, Oprah Winfrey sat down with Grammy and Oscar-winning musician and actor Lady Gaga for an intimate interview as part of the former's Vision Tour. The majority of the women's conversation centered on Gaga's chronic pain, which she attributed to the psychological result of the trauma of having been repeatedly raped years prior. In addition to talking about counseling and medication, the singer spoke at length about how she has embraced the concept of "radical acceptance" on her healing journey.

Lady Gaga confided that she has recurring episodes of being in so much pain she can only lie down on the floor and cry. From that place of desperation she often prays, "Thank you, God, for this pain. I surrender it to you. This pain is meant for me in my body right now. I'm here in this moment and I'm learning. Thank you for teaching me."[1]

The singer reported not only growing in self-compassion and empathy for others through this radical acceptance but actually seeing her symptoms begin to subside as well. (It's important to note that she is not saying God gave her the pain but that the pain is an opportunity to practice surrender.)

I've never experienced chronic pain, but when I watched this interview, I felt a sense of solidarity. Despite genuinely loving my role as a mom, raising five young children has been a source of significant stress, with occasional bouts of suffocating panic for me. I realize it might sound tone deaf to compare someone's trauma-based physical pain to the struggles of motherhood, but suffering is not a competition. Your hardship is legitimately hard; there is no need to measure it against the hardship of another. And as I listened to Lady Gaga describe her episodes of being laid out on the floor in debilitating head-to-toe pain, my first thought was, Yes, but at least you're alone. Ah, the mark of a well-adjusted human.

Radical acceptance of our present reality does not prohibit us from making helpful changes or advocating for our needs. We can't underestimate doing everything we can to prioritize our own physical, mental, emotional, and spiritual health. But there are some things that cannot be altered, some things that just . . . *are*. And after all our troubleshooting efforts are spent, we have access to inner freedom even when our circumstances remain unchanged.

It turns out Lady Gaga may have more theological insight than she is given credit for. Her message of radical acceptance echoes that of medieval saint and teacher Ignatius of Loyola, who placed great emphasis on what he called "indifference" or "detachment."[2] To this day, spiritual seekers all over the world—Catholic and otherwise—continue to experience vibrancy as they prayerfully follow his lead.

Ignatian spirituality teaches its practitioners to cultivate the inner freedom of remaining unattached to outcomes, whether those outcomes are how prayers are answered or how plans unfold. The Ignatian way seeks not to be tied to expectations but instead to trust that divine goodness is always present and available to us, ever ready to set us free from prisons of our own making. We are invited to hold the tension between what we think we want and what is currently being asked of us. So we begin to see that by forfeiting our resistance, we have excess energy to put toward communing with God, growing in freedom, and coming to greater self-awareness.

Training Your Brain to Hold Tension

One of my closest friends is a young woman ten years my junior. Allyson is single and not a mother, daring and brave, so I like to live vicariously through her many and varied adventures. A few years ago she participated in a ten-day meditation "sit" at a Vipassana center. Vipassana meditation is done in complete silence and requires the participant to sit still for hours at a time—up to ten hours a day!—focusing full attention on the experience of one's body and mind in the present moment.

It sounds extreme and, well, it is. But the people I know who have made it to the end of the ten days have sworn it is life changing, Allyson included. While I marveled how any human could possess the wherewithal to go unmoving for that length of time, she admitted it was not always pleasant (understatement of the year) but that she has seen the fruit of it in her everyday life.

One of the reasons Allyson was drawn to do the sit in the first place, she explained, was because the practice of meditation is not in keeping with her personality. She is an enthusiast, a traveler, a wild heart who often has more energy than she knows what to do with. But the shadow side of her vibrant personality is that she struggles to make space for more painful emotions—and not just her own, but those of loved ones as well. Allyson wants to make everyone feel happy and peaceful, sometimes at the detriment of inner growth.

As you can imagine, having to sit in complete silence and stillness for ten days was not easy. Welcoming every feeling she experienced, no matter how "negative," took practice. Sometimes it felt deeply rewarding. Often she wanted to quit. Holding the tension she was experiencing—in her physical body as well as in her mind—took a patience she hadn't been used to cultivating. But as days went by, Allyson began reprogramming her brain to respond to discomfort in healthier ways—feeling meaningfully present to the lows as well as the highs. At the end of her time, she noticed a difference and so has continued a modified form of the meditation.

With this practice, Allyson says, she has become more honest about difficult emotions, and that inner openness has extended to her relationships with others. Whereas before she rushed to "fix" uncomfortable emotions to regain a shallow sense of happiness, Allyson is now better able to stay present to the entire human experience, whether in herself or in another person, in the midst of difficult circumstances.

The way I see it, motherhood is like one long Vipassana sit. Over and over, millions of times and in millions of ways, we are confronted with extreme discomfort in our minds and bodies. Over and over again we are asked to stay—not just physically, but spiritually, mentally, and emotionally. Sometimes it feels rewarding and sometimes it feels unbearable. But through holding the tensions of motherhood, we have the opportunity to grow more welcoming to the movements of God in our life and in the lives of others.

Making Space for Discomfort

Our work is to neither run from nor fight against tension but to lean into it—to settle in, make friends with discomfort, and accept that our lives are not marked by dualities. We were not made for one thing rather than the other. We were made for complexity, for depth, for nuance: we were made for union with God, in whom there are unfathomable layers.

Just as I learned through yoga that my body's movements could rewire my brain, I have also experienced that rewiring my brain in turn rewires my soul. As we slowly stop programming our minds around fear and anxiety, we create space for curiosity and hope. When we let go of our expectations regarding outcomes, tension no longer has to feel like a threat to our well-being—or even our belief systems.

As our global consciousness grows at lightning speed, the millennial generation is finding itself confronted by rapidly changing ideas, theologies, and ways of being. It is an exciting time to be alive, in an era marked by emerging worldviews and a call to evaluate ideologies. This is a gift. But it can be confusing or scary at times, and we might feel threatened by having our paradigms challenged.

The remarkable thing about that fear-based, threatened feeling is that we have a choice in how we respond. We can unlearn the patterns that keep us defensive and suspicious. We can replace them with a generous spirit that assumes the best and a listening ear that seeks to understand and is even willing to be wrong. We can reprogram our brains to remain soft and open in places of tension.

Not only does this approach result in a less anxious experience but it also prevents walls from going up in our hearts toward those who see things differently. It keeps us gentle and teachable. In short, it produces the life of God within us. And no one is offered more physical opportunities to practice this spiritual reality than mothers.

⸺ Going Deeper ⸺

Take some time to search your heart and identify one area in your life in which you are experiencing the pull of tension. Perhaps it came to mind while you read this chapter; perhaps you'll need to dig a bit deeper to unearth it. What is one place you must acknowledge has no easy answers? (Examples might include the work-home balance, a crumbling marriage, an area of growth you're struggling in, or a shift in your belief system.)

Using your body to integrate your emotions, sit on the floor and straddle your legs wide. (Perhaps you feel a bit silly, and that's okay. Thank you for taking the risk with me.) Keeping that area of inner tension in mind, stretch to one side and let yourself feel the external tension your body will no doubt be making you aware of. Without pushing into the realm of pain, linger in the space of slight physical tension. Let your heart follow your body as your body becomes a living prayer.

As you stretch, breathe this prayer:

Thank you for teaching me to hold space for my discomfort without running away from it.

four

Reclaiming Solitude

Transforming Loneliness into an Inner Well

Mothering in the early years is a study in contrasts. You are almost never alone, yet you feel isolated. You are surrounded by people, yet these relationships are not reciprocal. Suddenly, after years of independence, you are now bound to the house for much of the day—bound to the haven of full-length naps and reliable snacks and the one place in the world where you know how to keep the ship sailing smoothly. Oh, you venture out, of course. You would go nutty if you didn't. But if you push too long you will pay the price. Your world becomes small, your circle in it even smaller.

That season does not last forever. Eventually life stops revolving around food and sleep, and it becomes logistically easier to reenter the land of the living. Yet when we finally dip our toes back into the social waters, we do so as different people than when we left. Many mothers find that the loneliness they assumed they would leave behind as their children aged continues to follow them through the years.

One would think the experience of motherhood is so singular that it would be relatively easy to forge deep ties with women who are going through the same thing. We imagine that other women have a ride-or-die group of besties whom they parent alongside, meet up with for playdates, and gather childless with for wine and cheese nights. And while some of us may be lucky enough to have such friendships with other moms, often the reality is less idealized than we would like to believe.

On the one hand, motherhood is a natural point of connection. A woman who is a mom can meet another mom for the first time on the other side of the world and easily make conversation for an hour. Years ago, before my husband and I had kids, we lived as missionaries in Southeast Asia, and I spent more than a little time jealous of the women on my team who had children because their connection to the local women was so effortless.

Now I enjoy friendships with Black mothers, Latina mothers, gay mothers, single mothers, Christian mothers, atheist mothers, anarchist mothers: the list goes on. I once participated in a prenatal class in which the facilitator said she believed that in her last life she was a cat. I have no paradigm for this, but hey, I was in a room full of mothers and was as happy as a clam. Motherhood is a social common denominator if ever there was one.

On the other hand, while it might be easy enough to establish surface-level connections with other moms, trying to go deeper can be a frustrating endeavor. For as much as we have in common, there is an expectancy that we will have *everything* in common. This is where our idealization breaks down.

Even among mothers who are the most like me (that is, white, middle class, married, straight, Christian) there are significant differences between us. Our marriages function differently. We are married to very different people. We have radically more or fewer children. Our children have special needs. Our children are in different stages of development. We have different theologies and politics. Our work-life balance looks different. Money is or is not a problem. We have different communication styles. The mere fact that we have both procreated is simply not enough to establish a deep heart connection.

We tend to look to other moms to understand us better than anyone, and it becomes painful when they can't. Mom-to-mom relationships are under tremendous pressure to satisfy our longing for friendship; more often than not, they can't deliver all that we want from them.

It turns out, if we are to be rescued from our isolation, it is not our mom friends who will be our rescuers. It will also not be our children, the attention of our partners, or the vibrancy of our faith communities, though such things are important and life giving. At the end of the day, there is no external relationship that can replace a woman's relationship with herself—the one companion she is guaranteed to have every day of her life.

In 2019, actress Emma Watson ignited a brief media stir when she referred to being single at thirty as "self-partnered."[1] While many leapt to applaud the empowering terminology, others responded with eye rolls and accusations of celebrity elitism. I admit the phrase sounded funny to me initially, but the longer I sat with it the more it resonated. I can't help wondering what would happen if all women adopted the perspective, regardless of relationship status. Can I, a happily married woman of nearly fifteen years, also be self-partnered? Can I identify as a fully whole individual who enjoys my own company while also not diminishing the very real value my significant other brings to my life? My gut tells me the answer is yes, and I'm learning that my gut rarely steers me astray.

Refocusing Inward

The fact that our loneliness is real and painful doesn't mean we are doing something wrong; it means we are human. Still, it is untrue to believe we have no agency in how we experience loneliness. When seen through the right lens, it may very well be our golden ticket to an exhilarating inner life.

As a celibate Catholic nun, author and social activist Joan Chittister knows a thing or two about loneliness. In her book *Between the Dark and the Daylight*, she details an early experience in her religious life as a student nun at age nineteen, living in a community of professed nuns who were all in their sixties. For various reasons, her elders were unable to offer Joan the meaningful connection she longed for. It was a lonely, desperate period of her life—a time she now describes as drowning in self-pity. Her loneliness was real and valid, but she eventually realized that the reason it was depleting her was not because loneliness is inherently that powerful, but because *she was giving it power*.

Chittister decided to use this temporary assignment as an opportunity to devote herself to interests she wouldn't normally have time to pursue. She studied all of Shakespeare's plays, learned to carve leather, and read every American musical, among other endeavors. She came alive artistically and intellectually in what had once seemed to be a hopeless situation.

Now if your family life is anything like mine, you probably aren't sitting around with a huge surplus of time and energy. Maybe the idea of studying Shakespeare for fun feels as implausible as taking a trip to the moon. There is a legitimate reality we bump up against, and that's okay. The point is not to fill your free time with challenging endeavors; the point is to explore your interests, desires, and personhood in an engaging and affirming way. The point is to fall in love with the woman you are.

Chittister writes, "Loneliness is a sign that there are whole parts of us that cry out for development. After all, we are meant to be more than our social lives. We are meant to have inner lives that are themselves rich and satisfying. It is a matter of learning how to become good company for ourselves."[2]

I, for one, have not always been good company for myself. That's a hard thing for a woman to aspire to when she has spent her life within a religious culture that convinces her that the definition of morality is to trust law above conscience and script above self; when she is part of a system that believes it has a fundamental duty to convince her she is innately flawed and has been so since birth; when week after week she is encouraged to second-guess her instincts and treat her desires with suspicion. How could I possibly be good company for myself when I was memorizing Bible verses like "The heart is deceitful above all things" (Jer. 17:9)?

No, I have not always been good company for myself. I have spent years asking God to change me, men to complete me, leaders to inspire me, friends to validate me, and community to sustain me. But there was a time in the beginning when this was not so. When I was a child, I would fill journal after journal with songs, poems, and fantastical magazine articles. I knew what it was to give way to myself, to dive deep and enjoy the swim in the waters that were mine and mine alone. I found my voice on the lines of those pages. I found myself, even before I knew what to call it.

As I aged I became aware that my proclivity for solitude was uncool. The right kind of girls went to parties and had boyfriends; they didn't eat chocolate in the bathtub every Friday night. My retreats inward went from being an exciting exploration to an embarrassing secret. I went to college to slough off my dead skin and see how a new one might feel. I partied dangerously and didn't care. I still had my journals and would write poetry when I wasn't drunk. In some ways I pity that girl, so far out of touch with her truest self. But in some ways I admire her, so brazen and willing to be wrong. She was a terrible mess, but she was her own mess. That's more than I can say for what came next.

It wasn't until I really got religious that I stopped writing altogether. For years I wrote neither poetry nor prose, my unconscious completely blocked by the overwhelming messages of the particular evangelical community to which I belonged. I noticed it, of course; noticed that I didn't seem to "need writing" anymore. *Must be because I have Jesus now*, I assumed. (As though I hadn't had him before. As though there aren't a million ways to have him.) *Must be because I'm healed.*

Years passed this way. I became a mother, and eventually it was motherhood that would compel me to leave that particular church—in search of what, I wasn't sure. I only knew I couldn't raise my son there. Within months I was writing again, and it's no kind of miracle except that it's enough of one for me.

Finding Your Passions

Not everyone experiences her soul through writing, of course. There are countless ways to spend time with ourselves, and another woman's way may feel as foreign to me as a different language. I've heard it said that we can find our true selves by looking back to the things we did instinctually as children, that often our juvenile pursuits serve as indicators of the activities that make us feel most alive, most connected to our Creator and Life Source. When I heard this theory presented, it was in the context of figuring out vocation. It's hard to argue with this logic when I grew up to be a writer, and my sister—who led many a summer classroom for the neighborhood kids and me—grew up to be a teacher.

But the principle can apply beyond the work we do. The activities that absorbed us as children can speak to the unique and particular way our souls were formed. I wrote poetry and prose as a child and have found the outlet to be in direct correlation to the condition of my inner life as an adult. Perhaps you spent hours making mud pies as a kid; have you considered gardening as prayer and soul care now—or the culinary arts? Maybe you laid in the grass and watched clouds morph into boats; when was the last time you pressed your body flat against the earth? Maybe you nurtured insects and animals as a child; have you tried letting nature's wild communicate with you as an adult? Did you sing and admire the sound of your own voice? Did you dance and feel liberated? Did you bicycle and know what it meant to soar? We may not all have such an archive of resources to look back on and draw from, especially those whose childhood was afflicted with trauma, but there may be more of a well there than you realize.

Those childhood markers of inner health are a great starting point when we're trying to reframe our idea of loneliness into one of solitude, but they certainly don't have to be the finish line. Think of them more as building blocks—*and then build on them*. Here is an inexhaustive list of ideas to experiment with in finding your own personal spirituality.

- *Take up a specific prayer practice.* Centering prayer is one many people swear by, but others that have stood the test of time are Ignatian prayer, Liturgy of the Hours, mindfulness meditation, and prayer beads (the rosary in my Catholic tradition, but Buddhism and Islam have their own variations too).
- *Make a point to regularly be present in nature.* While some people need a specific activity to focus on, such as gardening or running, it's often helpful to be present in the outdoors with no agenda at all. Sitting quietly or going for a leisurely hike can have astounding benefits for your spiritual imagination when undertaken as prayer.
- *Read insatiably.* I've come to believe that books have a mystical quality: they always seem to find us at the right

time in our life if we are open to their entry. Keep your eyes peeled and ears tuned to titles and descriptions that seem to resonate with something in your soul.

- *Try out a yoga practice to help you integrate body and soul.* We exist within a society that separates those two things, so we must intentionally work to restore the wholeness we were created for. If yoga is not your preference you might try Pilates, or one of the many similar adaptations available now.

- *Engage with the sacred writings of your spiritual tradition with a lens of self-trust.* This does not mean self-centeredness but rather a deep belief that the life of God is within you and you are perfectly able to interact with the divine without the intervention of someone else.

- *Pursue hobbies that surprise you.* Some of the most empowering experiences come from trying things we once assumed were not for us. Experiment with activities you feel drawn to but that no one has asked or expected you to do. (It's startling to realize how much we hold back because we are waiting for either permission or invitation.) Train for a marathon, take a painting class, or learn to play an instrument. Do something that scares you a little and you might be surprised by the woman who shows up.

Learning to Listen

Jewish feminist Hélène Cixous writes, "We must learn to speak the language women speak when there is no one there to correct us."[3] How do we learn that language? The same way we learn any language: by listening to it, over and over and over again.

Ah, you are thinking, *but I have no time to myself. I'm a mother, remember?* Yes, you are a mother, swimming in needs, paddling the kayak of your person through laundry and meals and dentist appointments. You once enjoyed hours on end to yourself, and you will one day again, but for now it is true that your margin of free time is thin. But remember this: *you are a world all your own*. No number of children, no bulging calendar, no teetering work-home balance can deny you that. There is a universe of mystery inside of you waiting to be unlocked. Listen to the woman within.

Listen to her in the mundane. Listen to her while you do the dishes. Listen to her instead of scrolling through your phone while your children play. Listen to her while you brush your teeth. Listen to her when you are pulling weeds. Listen to the language that women speak when there is no one there to correct you.

Listen to her when you make decisions. Listen to her when choosing which lullaby to sing as your little ones fall asleep. Listen to her when you choose a movie to watch after bedtime. Listen to her when you grab a book at the library. Listen to her when you make love. Listen to the language that women speak when there is no one there to correct you.

Listen to her when you experience emotions. Listen to her when your anger simmers but your lips stay sealed. Listen to her when desire swells. Listen to her when your curiosity is piqued and teased. Listen to what makes you cry. Listen to the language that women speak when there is no one there to correct you.

Listen, and believe what you hear.

—— Going Deeper ——

Sit in stillness for a few minutes and think back on your childhood. What was the language you spoke when there was no one around to correct you? How did your soul communicate itself to you? When did you feel most connected to God and the transcendent?

Give it time. If something comes to mind, make note of it. If nothing does, continue to think on the question as you go about your day. Pray for the Spirit to remind you of how your heart sang in the past. You might reach out to those who knew you well in childhood—parents or grandparents, siblings or best friends—to see what they remember. (But keep in mind your inner well of solitude may not have been witnessed by anyone else.)

If you can remember specific things, ask yourself questions about how those might be translated into an outlet for your adult self. If you can't remember anything, that's okay. In either case, you're going to want to expand your horizons eventually anyway. If your childhood self is inviting you to something specific, take that path with curiosity and delight. If your adult self is the only one making her desires known, that's fine too: experiment with those nudges.

And practice, practice, practice listening to the woman-language within you.

five

Following Anger

The Redemptive Power of Outrage

A few years ago my sister was in town for a visit, and we decided to take the kids to the park. Now I don't know about you, but in the parenting lobe of my brain I keep two distinct columns: things to do with the kids that require shoes and things to do with the kids that do not require shoes. I then choose accordingly. Going to the park is one of the few activities that floats between columns based on my level of energy and concern for social acceptability on a given day.

This time, my mom-game was strong enough to require that everyone wear shoes to the park. I bent low to adjust Taavi's Velcro straps, while Oscar climbed my back like a jungle gym. It had been a stressful morning, and I very much did not want to be touched—much less used as an obstacle course—but I was bearing it calmly. Yet when Taavi's frustration with my choice of shoes caused him to react by yelling out, "I hate these shoes!" and throwing one across the hall, I snapped.

"FINE!" I yelled back, my explosive volume shocking everyone. "DON'T WEAR ANY SHOES THEN!" Recovering my cool (and likely experiencing a bit of catharsis from my outburst), I immediately took a breath and lowered my voice, "I'm sorry, buddy. Here, let me help you find the shoes you want to wear today."

Across the room my sister raised her eyebrows and fought back a laugh. Seeing that I was ready to laugh too, she proceeded to voice her observation. "Geez," she smiled at the kids, "what makes your mom so scary is that she's so sweet and calm and then suddenly she yells like crazy, then immediately becomes sweet and calm again." The two older boys thought this was hilarious.

"Yep!" my son Moses agreed, laughing gleefully. "Mommy's like, 'arrrrgggghhhh!' like a monster for one second, and then she goes back to being really nice again." My oldest, ever conscientious of not hurting anyone's feelings, couldn't resist joining in: "But you never know when it's going to happen," Alyosha ribbed shyly. We all laughed, and I had to admit it was true. Even I didn't know when the rage that always bubbled underneath the surface would be unleashed. All I knew was that I should stuff it back down as quickly as possible when it did.

Our Anger Tells a Story

Generally speaking, as women, we are not comfortable with our anger. We go to great lengths to avoid even acknowledging when we feel angry, instead choosing less threatening words like *frustrated* or *sad* to describe our emotions. I cannot tell you how many times the fire of rage has been burning in my gut and yet the words that have come out of my mouth have been, "I'm not mad, but I *am* frustrated!"

Women are socially conditioned not to exhibit signs of anger—or perhaps more honestly, not to feel our rage at all. But we are human. Anger is a human emotion, neither good nor bad in and of itself, and a human being repressing a genuine emotion for years on end is never going to be very healthy or whole. Even aside from the social, emotional, and relational effects of anger on well-being, studies show that internalized anger leads to medical conditions like depression, anxiety, recurring headaches, and chronic physical pain.

When I say women are socially conditioned to repress anger, I don't mean we are absolved of our participation in that dysfunction; we do have agency in our choice of response. But I'm not sure we are able to examine our own complicity until we have reckoned with the massive number of unspoken rules about what is and is not appropriate for women to say, think, do, or feel—rules that have been set in stone for generations and that have informed the way our own mothers, grandmothers, and great-grandmothers were raised—and how they in turn raised us.

We females learned long ago how to play the hand we were dealt. We know our anger is not safe. Show me a demonstratively angry woman, and I'll show you a woman who has been deemed unhinged by those around her. Unlike the cooperation and somber respect garnered by men's anger, the demonstrated anger of women results in our being taken less, not more, seriously. Black and Latina women are given absolutely no margin of error on this. Most women from across racial backgrounds acknowledge that there are real social and relational consequences of expressing anger, and we calculate them in milliseconds before we even understand what we are doing.

Mothers especially are expected to be likeable, patient, and calm at nearly all times. We know this is unreasonable, of course, but as a society we don't want to see any evidence of a mother's temper. Maybe she does yell at her kids behind closed doors, but as long as it is not witnessed in the middle of Walmart we can continue on with our idealization of Madonna and Child.

Some of us have no recollection of ever seeing our mothers get mad, and we've all known men who gush over how saintlike their wives are or mothers were.

One night in 2019, Eric and I were up late watching one of our favorite mindless pleasures, Jerry Seinfeld's Netflix show, *Comedians in Cars Getting Coffee*. In this particular episode, actor Alec Baldwin sat across from Jerry in a diner and waxed poetic about what an absolute angel his wife was to "put up" with him. (One had to wonder what exactly the poor woman was putting up with.) I rolled my eyes at hearing this tired trope, then felt relief when Jerry Seinfeld shook his head and abruptly shut it down: "Nah, I hate that kind of talk. We're all just putting up with each other!"[1] Eric turned to me and we laughed because, *yes*, so much of coupledom is about just putting up with each other. If there is one party who is pulling significantly more weight in the "putting up with" department, the relationship is in need of an overhaul.

Instead of praising a woman who will toe the line and repress any inconvenient feelings, it's time we start poking holes in the narrative. Why *doesn't* a woman express unsavory emotions? Why *doesn't* she raise her voice or hold her ground? Perhaps to do so would be socially, emotionally, or even physically risky. Perhaps to do so would go against the religious ideal of submission she was raised to believe is obedience to God. Perhaps she is so far out of touch with herself she doesn't even know she's mad. Perhaps she has gotten so used to playing the game that she has perfected the art of subtle manipulation instead.

Our Anger Is Not Unjustified

In her national bestseller *Rage Becomes Her: The Power of Women's Anger*, Soraya Chemaly notes that there is one exception to this taboo: women are allowed to get mad on behalf of others. In fact, we may even be praised when we dig in our heels to advocate for our children, community concerns, or certain issues of social justice. The world loves a good Mama Bear story, does it not? But when we dare to funnel that rage into standing up for ourselves and our own best interest, we see just how quickly physical and metaphorical doors begin to close in our faces.

Chemaly's research also indicates that when our feelings of anger and resentment are attached to giving birth and motherhood, women are even more likely to repress them *and interpret them as a personal failure.* "Because these feelings are tied to motherhood, a role that is supposed to make us happy, peaceful, grateful, and fulfilled, they are doubly stressful and anger provoking. Motherhood, the ideal, renders these feelings illegitimate," she writes.[2]

But mothers have a lot to be angry about. Beyond the normal wear and tear of family life, mothers may also be carrying trauma related to childbearing. Infertility, miscarriage, infant loss, traumatic childbirths, adoptions, abortions, and unplanned pregnancies can be life-altering events, and yet few of us give ourselves the time, space, and permission to seek out the counseling we need. The world expects our grief to be private and brief, and we acquiesce. After all, our emotions are loose cannons, and no one wants a woman who is any kind of loose. We tuck our pain quietly away, where it simmers just under the surface.

And reproductive trauma is just the beginning. One in three of us were sexually abused by the age of eighteen. One in four of us have been physically abused by a partner.[3] And countless others have been victims of emotional, verbal, and spiritual abuse. But women suffer in unexceptional, everyday ways too.

We may feel stuck in unhealthy marriages because of financial dependence. We are usually carrying an inequitable amount of household labor and stress. We may have given up careers, willingly or unwillingly, for the sake of motherhood. We are not receiving equal pay for equal work. We may be sexually harassed in the workplace, or for that matter, on a walk around our neighborhood. We who are racial or sexual minorities face daily discrimination and prejudice. We may be in religious traditions that are male-centric and in which we feel unrepresented and powerless.

Yes, women have a lot to be angry about. And if we leave it unexamined, this anger can become toxic: it destroys relationships, stifles spiritual growth, and leaves us with a gnawing sense that we are wasting our lives.

But what would happen if we got curious about our anger, if we decided to follow it for a while and see where it leads? What might the anger of women—of mothers—have to teach us about ourselves and our societies? What if, as author and activist Austin Channing Brown has said, "Your anger points to what is wrong and what could be made right"?[4]

Our Anger Can Give Us Insight

A few years ago I was in a hard place. I had unexpectedly gotten pregnant before my then-youngest was even a year old. Meanwhile, our family moved twice in one summer. The stress had taken a toll on our marriage and on our children's behavior. I was spiritually parched, a foreigner to my own soul, and resentful of what motherhood was demanding of me. I loathed feeling like a victim of my own life yet felt trapped in the cycles I'd created. I promised myself I would try *something*, so I contacted a spiritual director and began meeting with her monthly.

I cried straight through the first two sessions. I had so much grief that stemmed from a disconnection from my true self: my needs, my desires, my embodiment. It felt like all my life amounted to was serving other people, and my Christian upbringing had convinced me that this was supposed to be a holy and satisfying calling—so why was I so miserable?

With the help of my seasoned spiritual director, I slowly began to admit that I wasn't just exhausted, disillusioned, bored, and resentful; I was actually very angry. And I was expending a significant amount of energy trying to convince myself and everyone else that I wasn't.

On one particular morning early in this journey, I wiggled around in the armchair in my spiritual director's living room. Tucking my knees underneath me, then pulling them back out again, I mused out loud: "Maybe I'm supposed to grow in accepting the present, to stop feeling so resentful and work on feeling grateful for my life."

She smiled supportively but cut through the malarkey in the way that only a seventy-year-old woman can. "I think it would be a good idea to stop assigning value to your feelings. What if you could see your feelings as information rather than as something you need to overcome? What if you let those feelings point you to your unmet needs—and then you were free to explore ways to meet those needs?"

My mind was blown. It had never occurred to me that trying harder might not always be best. Sure, it hadn't gotten me very far in the past, but wasn't that sort of the reality of life for everyone? You keep trying harder to be better and you fail most of the time, but maybe by the end you will have made a little progress? It looks pretty bleak when you spell it out this way, but tell me it's not how most of us live our lives.

With the invitation extended, I began learning to interpret my emotions as data to inform me rather than as indictments of some grave moral failure. It was through this daily practice that I came to terms with the fact that I was indeed pretty angry—and, more important, that there was nothing wrong with this. Facing my anger gave me powerful information about myself.

I was angry that my younger self had breezed through college, chosen the major that required the least amount of work, and graduated with no concrete plan of how to use my degree.

My immaturity then made it difficult to find gratifying work now, and it was okay to be angry about it.

I was angry that I had gotten married while deeply enmeshed in a church community that idealized stay-at-home mothers, and that I had unconsciously bowed to that position without any critical thought of whether it was what I wanted. My sense of self had been manipulated by those in authority, and it was okay to be angry about it.

I was angry that despite now wanting to work outside the home, I was virtually unhireable because I had been out of the workforce for years, found myself accidentally pregnant, and couldn't afford childcare. The deck was stacked against forging a new path for myself, and it was okay to be angry about it.

I was angry about a whole heap of other stuff too, but you get the gist. The anger inside that had gone unexamined had grown into a thorny resentment piercing the otherwise loving and delightful relationships I had with my children and partner. I felt trapped, even if among people I adored: trapped by the choices I myself had made more than a decade earlier.

When I followed my anger back to see its root causes, I was then able to take my spiritual director's advice and look for the unmet needs that were screaming for attention. By that point, it didn't take much soul-searching to realize I needed meaningful work outside of my role as a mom. Once I found a way to actively prioritize this, the lost pieces of myself began to snap back into place. It wasn't always a breeze—I wrote most of my first book with my newborn son Oscar either at my breast or sleeping beside me—but it was the start of a new way of being.

Our Anger Can Propel Us Forward

Sue Monk Kidd speaks of transfiguring rage into outrage. Rage is internal: a ball of fiery emotions held captive within us that,

left to simmer too long, can lead to physical and psychological ailments and bitterness. What rage needs, she says, is to
be transfigured into outrage. Kidd writes, "Outrage is love's
wild and unacknowledged sister. She is the one who recognizes
feminine injury, stands on the roof, and announces it if she has
to, then jumps into the fray to change it. She is the one grap-
pling with her life, reconfiguring it, struggling to find liberating
ways of relating."[5]

A prolonged nursing of our anger is never going to get us
anywhere. Yes, it's important to spend time with rage, acknowledge it, and explore it, but becoming overly sympathetic to our
own plight is not likely to inspire lasting change. When we have
grappled with our true self, feeling all our big true-self feelings
for long enough, we must then channel our potentially paralyz-
ing rage into an active, workable, empowered outrage.

Outrage is not a personality trait. Women with all different
temperaments can transfer their rage into outrage—and do
so in vastly different ways. Outrage does not equal yelling or
screaming or physical aggression. Being outraged means waking up, becoming disturbed by the status quo, and acting on
behalf of yourself to seek your own wholeness. Your anger does
not get to steer the ship, but it can be an illuminating lighthouse
to help you find the shore.

— Going Deeper —

Take a comfortable seated position and check in with your
physical body. Are you clenching your jaw? Shrugging your
shoulders? Biting your lip? Go through your body head to toe
with the intent of relaxing any tension you've been holding. As
you spend time noticing how your body feels, inhale and exhale
mindfully as you remind each part to unclench and settle down.

Once you feel relaxed and free, think about the most frequent or intense anger trigger in your life right now. It may be strongest with your kids, at work, with family and friends, or in any number of other spheres. Identify where your anger seems to camp out, then begin to ask questions about it.

Where does this anger originate? How far back can I trace it?

Have I internalized a sense of shame or failure from the fact that I feel angry? What if I could release myself from that?

If anger always points to an unmet need, what am I in need of that I am not getting?

What is one specific action I can take this week to move toward getting that need met?

six

Staying Curious

Fearless Nurture of Our Spiritual Selves

"Curiosity killed the cat!"

Yes, this antiquated phrase has actually passed my lips, thrown in the direction of one of my children in a moment of annoyance over the constant barrage of questions from not just one kid but five of them. The moment I spoke it I was already cringing. *Curiosity killed the cat?* What am I, a crotchety Depression-era grandmother?

Having talked with many moms about it, I know I'm not alone in this. Most of us have been guilty of stifling the creative energy of our little ones on a somewhat regular basis. When our babies are about six months old, we begin to discover that the ease of our lives will now have an inverse correlation to the curiosity exhibited by our children, so it's no wonder our knee-jerk reaction is to discourage said curiosity from the precocious little cherubs. *No, I can't explain to you how water towers work; we've got to keep walking if we're ever going to get to the park. No, I don't want to see what happens if we*

61

keep digging this dirt tunnel; it's making a huge mess. No, I haven't wondered what I might find if I search through the junk pile at the end of the neighbor's driveway; that would be really awkward.

But at some point we realize raising human beings is never going to be a convenient endeavor. One of the profound gifts that children bring is the slow, agenda-free pace wherein curiosity can flourish. Children put on the brakes, question things a thousand times, and force us to quit barreling through the one and only life we've been given.

So we google water tower facts, we keep digging the haphazard dirt tunnel, and we plunder the neighbor's trash. (Okay, maybe.) And the more we say yes to the curiosity of our children, the more we realize we also have permission to say yes to our own curiosity: a permission slip that doubles as a ticket to a more awakened spiritual life.

The interior life of children is innately mystical. It's a small tragedy that we spend so many hours instilling absolutes into our kids through religious education classes when they are the ones closest to God and should probably be teaching us the ways of their mysticism instead. In most Christian traditions young children are not allowed to participate in Communion until "the age of reason," but a more logical rule would be to let the pure-hearted toddlers have at the bread and wine and restrict access for the rest of us. Let the age of unreasonableness mirror back to us a wilder God.

Motherhood is a treasure trove for the spiritual pilgrim in part because we find ourselves in relationships of surprising reciprocity with these little people whom we thought we were supposed to guide and mold. Following my children's insatiable appetite for the divine has made me ache with the memory of what that was once like—and ache even more to find it again. Like the time my oldest son, Alyosha, asked me at three years old, "Mama, do you ever wonder how God is doing?" and I went to my room and cried like a baby because no, I didn't really wonder about that. I didn't really wonder about that at all.

The Wisdom of Asking Questions

Sadly, as we age our faith tends to narrow in on right belief rather than right practice. It gets harder to sustain that instinctual connection with our Creator after we become aware that there are entire institutions operating on the authority to determine who is in and who is out. It seems that entering adulthood all too often means becoming more concerned with knowing the correct things about God rather than experiencing God in authentic ways.

As a result, we might stay in the same church we grew up in because we are convinced it holds the only true doctrine; or we might wander from one denomination to the next—even one religion to the next—in search of apologetics that make the most sense. Neither of these paths is necessarily bad in and of itself, but what is problematic is a motivation of cognitive mastery. At the end of the day, right doctrine will not be enough to keep our interior fire burning. Right practice, however, can light a bonfire on the coldest night.

What do I mean by right practice? On the one hand, it's the specific prayer practices, mindfulness techniques, and sacred readings that resonate with you and anchor you to an experience of God that no outside voice can deny or diminish. The format of such practices will vary from person to person. On the other hand, right practice also encompasses a more general way of living that should be consistent among all people of faith: compassion, solidarity, mercy, justice, and awareness of the interconnection between yourself and every human and nonhuman life form.

The fact is, what is considered "right belief" changes over time and with context, even within the same religion. In Christianity alone, the idea of what constitutes orthodoxy has changed over the course of two millennia. Let's remember that Galileo's teaching that the earth revolves around the sun was declared heretical, and that the chattel slavery of African men and women was once vehemently defended as biblically justifiable. In our own generation, we have seen many denominations studiously and conscientiously change their doctrine on homosexuality from nonaffirming to affirming.

You see, right belief is not static. The perception of it has changed throughout human history and will continue to change as long as human beings continue to evolve. But right practice—the outworking of one's love for God and neighbor—never really changes. Young children understand this prioritization intuitively, even when their parents struggle to do so. A child is not likely to be impressed by a lengthy theological debate. But a child can recognize God at work when they see the hungry fed, the sick given medical care, and the poor sheltered.

Our kids are like miniature Buddhas, not just because of their chubby bellies but because they invite us to examine the details of this world with the love and wonder they deserve. The spirituality of children inclines them to care for the smallest things and to treat them with reverence. My son Taavi once picked up a worm and kissed it. I squirmed. He smiled.

But children don't just notice; they seek to learn. Their earnest desire to make sense of the world propels them to incessantly ask questions like *Why not? How come? What if—? What happens when—? Why? Why? Why?* Children, unlike adults, are never satisfied with being told, "That's just the way it is!"

I wonder what would happen if we digested these questions as a form of instruction for our own spiritual lives? What if we took our theological views or our political and social views and held them up under the microscope of our children's inquisitiveness? What might change, evolve, or broaden if we began pelting previously unquestioned beliefs with questions for the first time? Could it result in a life of greater love and awe? Could this be the childlike faith that Jesus preached?

Testing Boundaries

When I was in college and active in an evangelical church, a cautionary saying made its way through crowds like mine: "Don't be so open minded that your brains fall out!" I didn't just hear this admonition once; I heard it many times and in many settings. Now that I'm inching toward forty, I have more clarity on the inner movements and motivations behind my younger years. It's clear to me now that my biggest fear then was stepping outside the permissible bounds of belief that had been established by those in authority. (In Christianity, what this really means is the fear of going to hell, but that has a sort of crassness about it that makes people bristle, so it usually goes unsaid.)

Allowing someone else to draw boundary lines around your spiritual life is damaging. There is not enough emphasis on the abuse of this practice in religious circles, largely because boundary lines give us such a comforting (though false) sense of safety. It's like the analogy of the frog boiling to death in a pot of increasingly hot water: little by little, you get so used to distrusting yourself and pleasing others that you don't even realize that you are allowing your own peril.

In her book *Worth It*, pastor and author Brit Barron asks, "Is my life a reflection of who I want to be or a reaction to people I don't want to upset?"[1] When all the nuance, variation, and expansive vision that reside within your personal spirituality are forced to go through someone else's strainer, the really good stuff is never going to make it through their tiny filtering holes. You then lose the ability to create a spiritual life that reflects the person you want to be, and your relationship with God becomes mostly about the people you aren't willing to cross.

Refusing to let my spirituality be informed by fear has been a long process, but this first became important to me when I realized that such rigid control was simply inconsistent with the experience of the all-loving Goodness whom I had known. First to go was the fear of eternal damnation, then the fear of being wrong, and finally the fear of being disapproved of by others for my spiritual beliefs and practices. It is impossible to grow if you're too terrified to explore anything new.

It has been a journey, and there is a part of me that misses the certainty that marked my younger, more zealous spiritual experience. Because, after all, certainty feels safe. Certainty feels comfortable. There is not much that is comfortable about embracing an evolving theology—at least not at first. But it is normal, healthy, and good for us to grow into our understanding of the divine. What a shame it would be if we saw the Holy Eternal exactly the same at eighty as we did at twenty! That would indicate an entire life of missed growth. What a tragedy.

Although none of us wants to admit we have ever been wrong, none of us comes into this world fully evolved either. To grow in spiritual understanding we must reckon with our human need to wrestle, examine, and shift—and eventually see this as an invitation into a more abundant life. Curiosity asks questions with the intention of learning, rather than in anticipation of forming a well-crafted rebuttal. When we explore the feelings aroused in us by the "threat" of change, we learn to follow those feelings to find what God might be revealing through them.

Hearing Other Voices

On the journey of following our curiosity and allowing it to stretch us, dialoguing with and learning from other religious traditions can be invaluable. Contemplative author and scholar Beatrice Bruteau writes that interfaith exchange can revitalize a flagging spiritual life. "If one's faith has become too familiar, too flat, too routine, this may spark it afresh," she says. "If it has become too irrelevant, too incredible, too naive, [conversing with other spiritual traditions] may reveal its hidden depths and truer meanings, its capacities to challenge and to speak meaningfully to our time and place."[2]

I have found this to be true. Whether visiting Hindu temples, reading Sufi mystics, or listening to podcast interviews with rabbis, drawing from the wisdom of other traditions has bolstered my own personal adoration of God. In my twenties I avoided such things out of fear of being negatively influenced by them or even, in my wariest days, fear of opening the door to demonic possession. But now I'm grateful to have left those fears behind, because seeing the divine through new contexts and colors has resulted in a more satisfying spiritual experience. God is vast; no single tradition can contain the fullness of a limitless thing. We need one another's perspectives.

Even so, there is something to be said for digging deep within one spiritual tradition. There's a popular analogy among Buddhists that if you want to find water you don't dig six 1-ft. wells, you dig one 6-ft. well. In this sense, interfaith dialogue might be a way to sharpen our shovels—or trade in for a new shovel completely—but it is not equivalent to the actual work of digging deep in one chosen spot. Christianity is my well to dig, and the further I plunge into the works of contemplative thinkers and prayer practices within my tradition, the more living water I find.

This analogy came to mind as I read Mirabai Starr's book *Wild Mercy: Living the Fierce and Tender Wisdom of the Women Mystics*.[3] Starr, a modern Jew, does a fascinating job of drawing from female spiritual teachers of all religions: some dead, some mythological, and some living. I was educated and energized by being introduced to the wisdom offered from Zen priests and Hindu goddesses, among others, but what refreshed me most was reading insights about some of my favorite female Christian saints from a non-Christian perspective. By the time I finished the book, I found I loved Christianity far more—not less—than when I started.

Following Our Hearts

"Do you think we will ever become Catholic?"

It was 2010 when Eric asked me this question out of thin air. Knowing he had studied and been shaped by Thomas Merton, Henri Nouwen, and other Catholic contemplatives, I wasn't necessarily surprised by the question itself as much as by the timing of it. We were, after all, living as evangelical missionaries in Southeast Asia.

Unlike Eric, I had never spent significant time with Catholics, either in person or in books. The idea of shacking up in the Catholic Church was about as far off my grid as it possibly could have been. But having no real reason to shoot down the idea, I reached for the nearest strawman argument I could find.

"No, sorry, I don't think we ever will. I feel too uncomfortable with the whole Mary thing."

Fast-forward a mere four years, and a priest was making the sign of the cross on my head with holy oil and offering me the body and blood of Christ.

There were two seemingly opposing forces at play in my eventual conversion: the cosmic allure of mystery and the attraction of hard and fast answers. Today, the mystery touched on by Catholicism continues to have its hold on me, but I am less impressed than ever with the determination to lay claim to all the answers. When Eric and I entered the Catholic Church a friend told us, "I don't love everything about Catholicism, but everything I love is Catholic"—and even as a writer I can find no better words to sum up my own relationship to the institution. So here I remain.

Ironically, given our rocky start, the greatest gift Catholicism has given me is Mary. The Blessed Mother. Holy Virgin. Nuestra Señora de Guadalupe. The New Eve. Mediatrix. Stella Maris. By whatever name she is called, her universal feminine power is invoked, balancing an appallingly male-dominated religious tradition with the inclusivity, compassion, and generativity of a woman.

As I've grown into noticing the suspicious elimination of females from nearly all major religious narratives, the presence of Mary has become an increasingly necessary lifeline keeping me tied to the ship of faith. I wrestle with the patriarchy, misogyny, and patronization of women that marks the structural format of Catholicism (and, to be fair, most Protestant Christian denominations as well), but the companionship of the Mother of God has empowered me to resist succumbing to despair. At the time I ingested my first Eucharist, the Blessed Virgin was a part of Catholicism I begrudgingly tolerated. Years later, she is what keeps me here.

The details of that journey are for another day, but it goes to show how our spiritual paths are always winding. Digging in our heels in refusal to consider foreign ideas today might keep us from accessing the very thing that could save our faith tomorrow.

One night in the summer of 2020, as I rocked Oscar to sleep as I did every night, my free hand searched behind me for the wooden rosary I kept looped around the back of the chair. Praying the rosary had become a nightly ritual of mine, but I found it especially necessary on the days I had no words of my own to pray. This was one such day.

The Louisville police officers who killed Breonna Taylor in her home months before had still not been arrested. My social media feed was filled with Turkish women desperate to alert the world of the femicide taking place in their country. Congresswoman Alexandria Ocasio-Cortez was just cussed out by

Congressman Ted Yoho on the steps of our nation's Capitol. One of my best friends was recovering from an emergency hysterectomy following the traumatic birth of her twin daughters. The pain of my fellow women was devastating, and my heart had been especially heavy lately, but I wasn't consciously thinking of any of this as I circled the rosary with arms wrapped around my sleepy young son.

Fingering the little round beads, I began praying the first decade, or one set of ten Hail Mary prayers: "Hail Mary, full of grace, the Lord is with thee. Blessed art thou among women and blessed is the fruit of thy womb, Jesus. Holy Mary, mother of God, pray for us sinners now and at the hour of our death. Amen."

I did the first three recitations just fine, allowing my brain to travel to a space of peaceful meditation. At the end of the fourth time—in a glaring Freudian slip—I accidentally replaced *sinners* with *women*: "Holy Mary, mother of God, pray for us women now and at the hour of our death."

Immediately, my heart bore witness. *Yes*, it echoed. *Yes, that is exactly what I wanted to pray.* I thought of each woman whose pain had been lodged in my unconscious all day, and gratitude welled up like puddles in my eyes. Had you told me five years before that my soul would be opened through the beads of a rosary I would have laughed you out the door. But here was my loving Mother, simultaneously consoling and emboldening me through the rhythm of tiny wooden orbs. Here I had never expected to be, but here I was all the same: integrated, whole, and spiritually attuned. Who would have thought that exploring something new could be so worth the risk?

Hail Mary, pray for us women. Pray that we might have the courage to be curious.

— Going Deeper —

Identify and take one actionable step to experiment with following your curiosity. If you enjoy reading, seek out an acclaimed book written on a spirituality other than your own. If you prefer to listen to podcasts, find one that gently pushes you out of your comfort zone. If you typically pray with the scripture of your tradition, see what happens when you use the sacred texts of other traditions in prayer.

Remember that staying open and curious does not mean you must permanently incorporate any of these things into your own spiritual life. You may very well choose to do so, but you may also find that the thing you tried is not for you. Remind yourself that there is no agenda here; this is simply an exercise in opening up to the expansiveness of God.

After your action has been taken, spend some time digesting it.

How did it make you feel?

What questions did it raise?

What would you like to learn more about?

What inner movements do you notice?

How might God have spoken to you in a fresh way through this fresh channel?

seven

Cultivating Patience

Holy Resistance in an Age of Rush

I wasn't expecting to see an exposed boob when I went to retrieve the mail one autumn day in 2019. But there it was in all its pink-nippled glory on the cover of *Image*, an art and literary journal I've subscribed to for years. Once my initial surprise passed, I was struck by the intimate familiarity of the photograph. A woman in a siren-red dress had fallen asleep while breastfeeding her naked young toddler, who had also nodded off midritual. The exhaustion of the mother leaked from the page the way the last drops of milk leaked from her emptied breast.

The image immediately brought to mind the words of Brie Stoner, musician and alumna of the Center for Action and Contemplation, that I had read a few months prior: "Where is the icon of the mystic with one baby on the hip, a toddler crying at their feet, cooking dinner with one hand, trying to finish work on a laptop with the other?" she asked. "Because *that's* my real life."[1]

While the particularities of motherhood depicted in artist Leni Dothan's *Sleeping Madonna*—represented on that magazine cover—are different from those requested by Stoner, the point is the same: women desperately need our lived experience reflected back to us in sacred ways. It is not enough to be given idyllic Renaissance paintings of Mary and Jesus or renderings of historical female saints looking demure and pious. Such idealization isn't always bad and can sometimes inspire, but if that's the only spirituality of motherhood we are handed, we will inevitably feel ashamed and isolated when our own experience is much less palatable.

As an Israeli-born Jewish mother, Leni Dothan has a vested interest in the customary portrayal of Mary and Jesus. In her *Sleeping Madonna* installation (which was originally a video on loop before it was a magazine cover), she says, "The iconic Mary becomes a real-life mother, weak and exhausted, unable to live up to her own myth."[2]

Unable to live up to her own myth. This is the myth of the ever-accessible mother: the mother who will always give tirelessly, smile tenderly, respond patiently, and accept the hand she has been dealt with endless grace and ease. It's a fiction, a caricature of a mother. It is not reality. Real mothers wrestle. Real mothers fail. Real mothers lose it, pick themselves back up, dust off their ego, hug their child, and try it again. Real mothers must learn to have patience with themselves just as they are trying to learn patience with their children.

Granting Ourselves Some Grace

Ask any mother to list the ways in which she most needs to grow, and patience will almost assuredly be named. Moms all know that to nurture our little ones well over the span of many years, patience is a basic requirement—and yet we always feel we're coming up short. I wonder if there is a spiritually minded mother on the planet who has not prayed to have more patience with her kids.

The thought brings to mind a scene in the movie *Evan Almighty*, where Morgan Freeman, who plays an embodied God, asks Lauren Graham, who portrays a distraught wife and mom, to reconsider her understanding of prayer. "Let me ask you something," he says, under the guise of a restaurant worker, "If someone prays for patience, do you think God gives them patience? Or does he give them the opportunity to be patient? If someone prays for courage, does God give them courage, or does he give them the opportunity to be courageous?"[3]

We can beg and plead in prayer to be supernaturally changed into women who suddenly have the mental bandwidth for childish foolishness. We can moan and groan about how we need to do better, how we *must* do better; we can chastise ourselves for still being impatient after all these years. We can make all these appeals; and yet, call me a heretic, I don't believe God can do much with all that.

Don't get me wrong. I believe prayer wields a lot of power. When we pray for something virtuous and right—like to have more patience with our kids—we open ourselves up to a dynamic spiritual energy, because God is really in agreement with this wonderful longing we have. But the shift doesn't come in the form of us being magically changed overnight; the shift comes in the grace to set patience before us as an intention. *Patience is something we must practice.*

The word *intention* is used slightly differently depending on the crowd you find yourself in at a given time. For most of my Protestant Christian life, *intention* was used only in nonspiritual ways to communicate the purpose or hope behind an action: "I'm sorry my being late caused you anxiety; that was not my intention." On becoming Catholic I learned the word was interchangeable with what I had always labeled prayer requests: "I brought my list of intentions along with my Bible into the chapel." My favorite usage, though, is when the word comes up in my yoga class when the instructor pauses at the beginning of the session and invites us to set an intention for our practice that day.

Setting an intention for a predetermined length of time—say, during an hour-long yoga class or one single day at home with the kids—can be an effective way to focus on an area where we want to grow and to purposefully invite the Spirit into the process of our growing. I've found that keeping a candle lit helps me stay attuned to my intention, because every time I pass it throughout the day I am reminded to recenter and bring my thoughts and feelings back to the wholeness I'm hoping for.

When we set a specific daily intention, the manner in which we internalize it will determine its effectiveness. If you struggle to stay mindful and only berate yourself for getting off track, no good will be served, and you might even feel worse than before you started. Gentleness with self is the name of the game if you want to see fruit from this practice, but being gentle with yourself as a parent is difficult when you're raising kids in a day and age with sky-high expectations of mothers.

Even aside from social pressures, we sincerely want to be the mothers we believe our kids deserve. The thing is, sometimes that keeps us from being the mothers our kids *need*—which, I would argue, are mothers who demonstrate what it is to struggle, fail, recenter, and refocus. Our children are not going to grow up to be perfect themselves, so do they need an unrealistic model of flawlessness—or do they need someone to show them what it means to navigate their flaws with empathy and connection?

Buddhist priest Karen Maezen Miller reflects on the ways her spirituality affects her experience of motherhood in her insightful book *Momma Zen*, which is my go-to when I need contemplative recentering in my parenting. Drawing from her Buddhist training, Miller invites us to consider abandoning the idea of failure, suggesting that we might like the result a lot more if we cease the cycle of self-criticism altogether.

> All manner of events transpire in life, but where exactly does this thing called a *mistake* take place? Only in our mind—our judging, critical, labeling mind. The mind that provides the nonstop narrative to our lives: "There you go again. Can't get it right." . . . What is a mistake without the self-critical label? It is just what it is. . . . Life is full of fits and starts. Some things are easy; some are not. Some things go and some things stop. Do your work; then set it down. There are no failures. *Forgive and forget yourself.*[4]

If this sounds like New Age mumbo jumbo, I would mention that Buddhism was founded in the sixth century BCE. More to the point, the wisdom being offered here transcends any single spiritual teaching and permeates all contemplative traditions, even Christianity. Julian of Norwich experienced the same revelation during her third mystical vision of Jesus, of which she wrote, "I saw truly that sin is no-deed. . . . For since all things have their ground in God's making, so all that is done belongs to God's doing. It is easy to understand that the best things are well done: yet as equally well as the best and highest deed is done, so too is the least thing well done."[5]

I'm not sure that Julian of Norwich would observe me yelling at my toddler and respond with a high five and a "Well done!" I think her meaning here is on a more mystical plane, one in which any action we undertake can be trusted to find its wholeness in the expansive arms of God. The call for us in her words is to see that all that is done is now buried in the divine bosom. Or, as returning to Miller's words, "It is just what it is." No value, no judgment.

What might happen if we quit loathing ourselves for our parenting mistakes and choose to agree with both of these women that our actions judge us only to the extent that we let them? What kind of mothers would we be if we decided to treat *ourselves* with patience rather than condemnation?

Patience as a Spiritual Practice

There is something nauseatingly precious about the way we envision maternal patience. The picture painted is one of gentle murmurings, lilac flowers, whimsical rainbows—and more than a little bit of doormat syndrome. But the truth can be much different.

When practiced rightly, patience is a force to be reckoned with. It's revolutionary. Powerful. It is resistance. While the world around us blazes by, demanding consumption, greed, instant gratification, and self-interested exorbitance, the virtue of patience is downright prophetic in its refusal to bow to empire. It's like how gardening looks harmless and sweet while in actuality it is dismantling hierarchy, scarcity, capitalism, and environmental degradation. If patience was a hobby it would be gardening.

Happily, slowness is making a bid for reemergence these days: we see it everywhere from the fashion industry ("slow fashion" as the antidote to "fast fashion") to food production (farm-to-table fare instead of fast food) to recreation (popular new fads like "glamping"). It's no coincidence that increased global consciousness is at the heart of these changes; we can clearly see that many of our habits are not sustainable for either personal or collective health. The human race innately knows we cannot thrive for long by outpacing ourselves. We must relearn patience.

The environment is begging us to slow down. The poor and underserved are begging us to slow down. Medical professionals are begging us to slow down. Garment workers and farmers are begging us to slow down. Rain forests are begging us to slow down. Our children are begging us to slow down. Cultivating a spiritual practice of patience one day at a time, even one moment at a time, has the potential to spill over into every layer of society and carry with it the seeds of change that could very well save the world if each of us had this inner resolve.

Our need for more patience is not only about the way we relate to our children; it's not even mostly about that. We moms expend a lot of emotional energy on cultivating patience with our children: we commiserate about it in moms' groups; we read every parenting book under the sun; we shoulder self-imposed guilt; and we seek answers from mentors and therapists. And yet few of us put forth any effort to cultivate patience outside of our role as a mother.

But your motherhood does not exist in a vacuum; everything is connected. If you pray to become a more patient mother yet have not considered how to open up that stream to other parts of your life as well, you aren't likely to see much change. On the other hand, if you reframe the pursuit of patience to explore what it means to be a whole person who patiently finds her being in the world—including, but not limited to, your role as a mother—you might just find yourself on the cusp of a transformation. If you hope to be more patient with your child, you must also prepare to become more patient with your partner, yourself, your society, your earth, your ambitions, your body, and your work. It's the best game of dominoes you will ever play.

When we cultivate patience as a spiritual practice, we learn to love ourselves for our small but earnest attempts at self-betterment; in so doing, we learn to love those around us for theirs. We begin to believe that being is higher than doing, that awareness is higher than hustle. Radical patience says, "I will not be owned by another—whether mass marketing, family members, economics, or culture." Patience is stubborn, defiant, and unstoppable. Patience is a woman who belongs to herself.

Slow and Steady

Radically patient women change the world. Could Susan B. Anthony or Harriet Tubman have achieved justice for countless numbers of people without a spirituality of patience? Could Mary Oliver or Joy Harjo write poems without allowing time for those words to simmer and emerge? Could Dorothy Vaughn have computed NASA calculations by hand, knowing there would be no fruits from her labor for months or even years?

Most things worth doing don't yield quick results. Patience requires us to bow to the muse within—whether what she seeks is a right society, an unshackled creativity, or any number of other good things. We hold tightly to our dreams while relaxing our grip on their timeline. To be truly patient is to fight and surrender simultaneously.

A performance space director once quipped to the *New York Times*, "You can't paint at night in your kitchen and hope to be a good artist. It doesn't work that way."[6] When artist and mother of three Allison Reimus read those words, she was stunned by what they represented: the obliviousness of her male artist counterparts to the experience and very existence of women who make valuable art amid demolished Lego structures, muddy uniforms, and dirty diapers.

The male director's words propelled Reimus to juror the Artist/Mother Podcast's debut exhibition, cheekily titled *Painting at Night*, which featured women's art inspired by motherhood and domesticity and was displayed in the Fort Houston Gallery in Nashville in 2020. "We [artist/mothers] are well aware that the separation of the domestic from serious artistic inquiry is a patriarchal myth," she writes in the exhibition catalog. "May we all . . . continue painting at night and persist in creating our own opportunities when it feels like there is no room for us at the proverbial contemporary art kitchen table."

As mothers, we are tasked with following our ambitions and creative expressions in a more roundabout way than fathers or childless women have to do. For us there will never be enough time to devote to the art we want to make, the words we want to write, the business we want to start, or the activism we want to pursue. It will never make perfect sense. It will never be approved of by everyone we know. It will never feel like the best use of time.

Do it anyway.

Do it at half speed when you wish you could give it your all in one fell swoop. Do it bit by bit, knowing that in other circumstances you would have wrapped it up by now. Do it slow and steady, nice and easy, and shrug it off when people act like it's a cute hobby you have or a side gig. Let their attempts at diminishment slide off like water from a duck's back, because you don't have time for that mess. You are building and creating and dreaming and doing, and you've got school pickup at 3:30.

Your dreams, your work, your voice in this world are important. We need them. *You need them.* They will unfurl slowly, yes, more slowly than you might choose. But as you put them on pause to cook a meal or nurse a baby or console a teenager, remember that the time spent percolating is only going to make the idea better. In a world that pulls the trigger to produce quickly and efficiently, your work has had time to deepen and expand. When you physically put down your work to tend to the minutiae of life, you unconsciously bring the work with you; then, when you physically return to it, often you will see it differently. Good ideas are made better when dipped into real life now and then.

People tell you that necessity is the mother of invention; what they don't tell you is that invention thrives on limitation—and no one knows limitation like a mother.

We have to be willing to move slowly, we who paint at night in our kitchens in a million different ways. We have to be willing for our ventures to take longer than we would hope, to pause our work more frequently than we would like, to become more frustrated than we feel we can bear. But the patience we are asked to bring to our work is the patience we are asked to bring to our children, the patience we are asked to bring to our lives, the patience we are asked to bring to our earth. It is a spiritual patience, a spiritual discipline, and it births spiritual fruit.

When you paint at night in your kitchen at the table where your kids have thrown rice and dug into the wood with forks, the table that you have wiped down three times that day but somehow still has jelly on it, what has happened is that your life has seeped into the wood. And from that space you can bring all of the wisdom from your ordinary, extraordinary life into your creation, making it somehow more than the sum of its parts: making it touch the very connective tissue of what it is to be human, made of both soil and stars.

This is what others may not understand about painting at night. This is the magic of a creative motherhood.

— Going Deeper —

For one single day, set an intention of patience. Begin the day by lighting a candle and putting it in a place you will pass often. As you light the wick, take a few moments to breathe deeply, inhaling the presence of God and exhaling any sense of rush or urgency. Take a minute to do nothing but watch the flame.

Remember, you are deserving of patience. Look at yourself through the eyes of a mother for her beloved daughter and feel the compassion that arises for how hard you're trying. Invite that little girl to rest.

You will not maintain patience perfectly today. You will forget. You might lose your temper. You might feel hopeless.

Remind yourself that the goal of today is not perfection but compassion. Patiently trust the process; do not rush it. Today you have the chance to forgive yourself, have mercy on yourself, and model for your children what that looks like—so that one day they might know how to forgive and have mercy on themselves too.

Return to your candle and recenter a few times throughout the day. Let the flame remind you of the powerful work of resistance you are undertaking, a work that reaches far beyond the boundaries of your individual home. Breathe deeply and feel proud of yourself, not because you finally got it "right," but because you finally see the value in not having to.

eight

Heeding Intuition

Divine Movement through Feminine Wisdom

We've all heard the stories: like the one about the mother whose gut tells her something is wrong with her child despite assurances from doctors that all is well, only to have a cancer diagnosis once the tests she demanded are run. Or the mother who feels compelled to check on her sleeping baby at a random time of day and in doing so discovers a blanket wrapped around his neck. Or the mother who calls her teenage daughter at a party, not knowing she was being sexually pressured by a boy and wishing for a way out.

You've heard the stories. Maybe you've lived the stories. The folklore surrounding a mother's intuition remains steadfast even in our skeptical modern society. Even the least sentimental among us are likely to acknowledge that mothers possess some maternal instinct—frankly, we almost have to believe it: most of us have witnessed it first- or secondhand.

My own mother was efficiently notified in a dream when I had sex for the first time the summer after high school graduation.

A year later she was told in another dream what my future husband would look like. A year after *that* she called me from another city when I was alone in a hotel room with an older guy, and she even sensed I was lying when I pretended to leave but really had just gone out into the hallway. Looking back, I know that encounter would not have ended well; even though it was embarrassing at the time, I am now relieved that my mom sensed danger and made sure I walked away.

It doesn't always go this way, of course. Death happens. Sexual assault happens. Children suffer with no one seeing. As real as a mother's intuition is, the fact that it doesn't always manifest itself is a cruel fact of life. If only we could summon it on command. But we have to let life be life, even in its mysterious inconsistencies.

I gave my mom a run for her money when I was younger, so I like to think her subconscious is getting a break in my adulthood. These days Eric's mother is the one with the sharpened sniffer, always seeming to know when a change is coming or depression is hitting. She's so attuned that we're not even surprised anymore when the phone rings right on time.

Not all moms experience their intuition in dramatic ways; even still, it's present. It's what tells us this baby needs to nap against our breasts in the sling even when experts say he should be in a crib. It's what tells us our third grader needs to go to a physical school, even though her older siblings thrived in homeschool. It's what tells us when our teenagers need to be protected and when they need to be given the freedom to make mistakes.

Most of us have to grow into our mother's intuition. In my experience, it's rare to find a woman who is confident enough to listen to her own right off the bat; more often we listen to the advice of everyone else in the beginning, terrified of doing something egregiously wrong. Learning to trust ourselves as mothers is a slow, holy process.

As fascinating as the physiology of a mother is, maternal intuition is not necessarily biological. Yes, postpartum hormones have a place in teaching us how to care for and protect our newborn babies, but as someone who experienced motherhood before I had given birth, I can attest that the power of intuitive love is much more than brain-based chemical reactions. Each of us has a sacred wisdom inside to guide us in raising our children, regardless of what form our particular path to motherhood took.

As spiritually inclined women, we may have no problem attributing our intuition to a kind of God-speak. It makes sense that if the mystery of God is love, then the love we have for our children, coupled with our intimate connection to them, would be a powerful conduit of supernatural communication. But we might be surprised to learn that our theological traditions support this as being a specifically feminine outworking of God.

Intuition is a form of wisdom, and the Judeo-Christian tradition personifies Wisdom as female. Biblical literature calls her Sophia, which is Greek for "wisdom" (Prov. 8:22–31 is one example). Scripture tells us Sophia was with God at the beginning of creation; in several passages of the Old Testament, the delineation between Wisdom and God is blurry, often imperceptible.

Recognizing intuition as divine movement can help us trust it and act on it. Communing with Sophia is one of the ways we can learn to integrate the traditionally separate ideas of God and self. Jesus preached often about God indwelling people, but two thousand years later his followers relate more to God as a being "up there" than as residing "in here." Learning to trust Wisdom/Sophia rebels against that separation and brings our relationship with God nearer—more earthy, more intimate. Right down into our gut, exactly where Jesus would want it to be.

In our Western society, physical experience has been severed from spiritual experience. It's not just that we are an increasingly fact-driven people but that we are a sorely disconnected one. Our medicine, our religion, our education, and our social structures all either struggle or outright refuse to integrate the scientific with the supernatural. As a result we are highly suspicious of things like intuition, especially as a motivator for decision-making or anything else that carries high stakes. We do not trust intuition in ourselves, and we do not trust it in other people.

I can't help but think of the scene in the sixth Harry Potter movie when teenage Harry tries to convince two of his professors that his classmate Draco Malfoy is the culprit behind a cursed necklace. When asked for a basis for the accusation, Harry simply says, "I just know." If Harry represents us in the Western world trying to follow our intuition, then Professor Snape embodies the centuries of social structure we're up against when he curls his lip and sneers derisively, "You just . . . *know*."[1]

Our cultural norms cause us to belittle and distrust the very idea of intuition, with one notable exception: maternal instinct. We devour stories of the intuition of mothers, the more salvific the better, pulling the meat from the bones and licking our fingers afterward. We spin tales of a mother's intuition into movie plots, best-selling memoirs, and inspirational keynotes. We are insatiable because we are deprived.

But as with a woman's anger, modernity takes a woman's intuition seriously only if it is leveraged in defense of someone else. If a woman acts intuitively on behalf of her child, she's a hero. If a woman intuitively acts on behalf of herself, she's a joke. Why do we stand for that? Why do we allow our most intimate feminine wisdom to be mocked or called into question? Why are we brave when it comes to our children yet timid to be true to ourselves?

Why We Repress Our Intuition

Terry Tempest Williams, a naturalist, activist, Mormon, and celebrated author, writes in her book *When Women Were Birds*, "When we don't listen to our intuition, we abandon our souls. And we abandon our souls because we are afraid if we don't, others will abandon us."[2]

And that's it, isn't it? We are slow to trust our intuition because we've been told it's unsafe and imprudent to do so, that it is dangerous and won't be tolerated. Our mothers and grandmothers and great-grandmothers and great-great-grandmothers were told the same. We are afraid that if we don't abandon ourselves, others will abandon us, and this has often been accurate: in past ages, a woman's vulnerable place in society meant there were physically unsafe ramifications to trusting herself instead of those in power over her. This has been exponentially true for women of color.

So we betray ourselves in order to stay in the good graces of others—unconsciously trying to earn their love—whether in the form of patriarchal society, family members, friend groups, religious institutions, academia, or anything else. We lay down our sacred feminine wisdom, our ability to know and translate the God-speak within, at the feet of whomever can convince us they have authority over us, whomever can convince us that we cannot make it without them. And then we spend a lifetime wondering why we don't feel free.

Ah, *freedom*. That elusive word used to market and sell to weary women since the beginning of capitalism. The word we all thirst after. What does it even mean to be free? What must we shed to get there? In her book *The Star in My Heart: Discovering Inner Wisdom*, Catholic sister Joyce Rupp says inner freedom comes from trusting ourselves to follow the Spirit within. But freedom asks a price from us, and that price is usually related to our sense of security, certainty, and assurance of being right. "It often hurts to let go of what we thought was the truth," and continuing on she writes:

> There is some necessary purification involved when we let go of the ego's strong need for security. We must be willing to pay the price for inner freedom. Part of the cost for this is our willingness to surrender to Sophia's guidance and direction, to trust that she knows the way through the darkness. Will we trust Sophia's presence and light? Will we deliberately and intentionally pause to reflect on our feelings and motivations? Will we let go of what keeps us from being our truest self? Will we choose to move toward what gives life and not just toward what gives security? These are Sophia questions, leading us toward greater inner freedom.[3]

For too long women have compromised their sense of self for a sense of belonging. We have been told it is dangerous to trust ourselves, it is dangerous to listen to Sophia in our gut. We've been told we need a middleman (emphasis on *man*) to lead us to God. We've been told the gender injustices we experience daily don't exist. We've been told what our body shape and size should be. We've been told we couldn't possibly have been called to leadership. We've been told we are not as trustworthy as men. That we are not as smart. Not as rational. Not as holy. We've been told that we sinned first.

Reopening the Door

I have a large tattoo on the top half of my left arm—a "half sleeve," as they say. When I met with the tattoo artist for a consultation, I brought along the image that had inspired my idea: a print titled "Mary Comforts Eve," drawn by Sister Grace Remington of the Sisters of Mississippi Abbey in Dubuque, Iowa. The fact that I handed a twentysomething tattoo artist with a half-shaved head the work of a cloistered Cistercian nun and said something like "This, but make it edgy" tells you all you need to know about me really.

In the image, two women stand facing each other: one in a floor-length dress and blue head covering, the other naked, her long, dark hair falling in strategic places around her curves. They are Mary and Eve. Mary presses Eve's hand atop her own protruding pregnant belly, reaching out with her free hand to caress Eve's face in a gesture of tenderness. Eve, clutching an apple close to her chest, looks despairing. Below, a snake is wound around Eve's leg, but Mary's foot rests atop its smashed head.

Writer Laura Jean Truman describes the narrative of the painting this way: "While Eve can't even bring herself to make a move towards her own freedom, Mary takes Eve's hand for her. While Eve's body is heavy with shame, Mary doesn't force her to give up anything she's not ready to—she just invites her to touch what is new."[4]

I adore my tattoo. Like all good art, its meaning has evolved for me over the years. Initially, I loved the idea of telling the Christian story of redemption through an exclusively female lens, for it's not often that men are left out of that narrative. But over the years the mythological significance has captured my spiritual imagination in even more ways.

I'll be the first to say that cultivating a devotion to Mary has been transformational for me, yet I don't think this image is only about her. On a mystical level, I believe it's also about the two women within me. The sinner and the redeemer. The captive and the empowered. The one who internalizes shame and the one who declares there is no need. The one who can't let go and the one who invites her into freedom. Eve reminds me to have compassion on myself; Mary reminds me that I have agency.

The story of Adam and Eve is a loaded one. Every creation story offers much more than an idea of how the world began;

it tells something about the culture where it originated. And the biblical creation story says much.

The impact of the story of the Garden of Eden extends beyond the Judeo-Christian tradition. You would be hard-pressed to find someone in the Western world, whatever their religion or lack thereof, who is not familiar with it. For many of us, the story of Adam and Eve is a cultural origin story as much as it is a religious one. It's not surprising that wherever this story is told there is usually a patriarchal social order and an underlying belief that women are weaker, less trustworthy, and are to blame for the brokenness of the world. Even those of us who don't read the story literally have nevertheless been irrevocably affected by its interpretation, handed down to generation after generation for thousands of years.

These days, theologians are able to give clarifying explanations for what have long seemed to be sexist undertones in Eden. Lisa Sharon Harper points out that man was not created first; for example, the Hebrew word *adam* simply means "human being" and gender-neutral language is used on that human's creation. Harper asserts that when God sees the human being needs a companion, the *adam* is put to sleep, and God separates male from female just as God separates light from darkness. This is the first time we see gender-specific language for humans in Genesis.[5]

Regarding the infamous curse that a woman's husband will rule over her (Gen. 3:16), Harper says the declaration is *descriptive*, not *prescriptive*. In her book *The Very Good Gospel*, she writes, "Male dominance is nowhere to be found in the heart of God's intentions for humanity prior to the Fall. . . . God is simply describing the natural outcome of humanity's having broken the way to peace. Humanity chose the way of dominance. Between men and women, it takes the form of patriarchy, which shows what it looks like to live in broken shalom."[6] God's desire is for the human race to move toward the original oneness in Eden, not for us to defend and uphold the systems that were produced by sin.

As for that snake? I've been fascinated to find widespread scholarship affirming that because of its regenerativity in shedding its skin, the snake was an ancient symbol of fertility, sexuality, rebirth, and the forces of creative life: a symbol, essentially, of all that is feminine. Snakes were often depicted in divine feminine images, portrayed accompanying goddesses and such, and everyone living in ancient times would have made this immediate connection after hearing the Eden story, including its intended Jewish audience.

It's okay to stop here and grieve this. For Jews and Christians, it is painful to see how the religious traditions that have nurtured us into a love for God have also been so clearly formed and shaped by a patriarchal perspective. Whatever the author's original intention may have been, the narrative is most often read as an indictment of Eve. Since Eve was the one conversing with the snake, as well as the one who ate the apple first (with Adam right by her side, we are told), the story lends support to sexist systems and perpetuates ideas about female inferiority. The symbols of the story have been co-opted to restrain women, to make us less prone to acting from our gut. And it has been an effective strategy for a long, long time.

The biblical creation story emerged within a specific culture in an attempt to make sense of and create meaning within the world. It was told by human beings who were sincerely seeking the divine in the best way they knew how within a flawed human system, and that is a deeply holy thing. It's a sacred story, and I would never want to erase it. But I do think it's important to know what we're eating and how to chew our food, rather than just let ourselves be spoon-fed while blindfolded.

I still love the story of Adam and Eve. I still love my tattoo, even with Mary stepping on the head of the snake, because I want my mind to be stretched into thinking about my beliefs in a hundred different ways. After years of wanting certainty, I now realize I shouldn't presume to be certain about much when it comes to God. Rather, I want to be fascinated. And so I want my theology and mythology to be complex, layered, and complicated.

We can reclaim snakes as a sacred feminine symbol, *and* we can appreciate the story of Adam and Eve—we really can. Immaturity and dualism want to convince us otherwise, but the truth is there is room for all of it. As women, we need to be aware that our internalization of this creation story must be kept in check. No story of the life-bearing, generative, love-induced fertility of God *bringing us forth in the first place* should be allowed to make women (who reflect the life-bearing, generative, and love-induced fertility of God) feel that the deepest parts of ourselves are untrustworthy. As Austin Channing Brown says, we must "trouble the narrative."[7]

Intuition with Discernment

So can I indiscriminately follow every gut feeling I have? No. I am not an unvarnished vessel of communion with God. I am a flawed human being with nearly four decades of baggage, much of which shapes the way I see the world and the decisions I make on a daily basis. I can't trust every hunch I may have, for they are often inaccurate or incomplete.

This is the tricky part and what makes it so tempting to outsource our inner knowing to rules and authority figures instead. We each have our own traumas, fears, and shame through which we filter information. We each have bias and ignorance because of our limited life experience. These things don't make us bad or inherently untrustworthy; they make us normal human beings. But we can't just blithely accept our condition; we have a responsibility to discernment and to growth, to self-awareness and to education.

In Catholicism we hold to the primacy of the conscience, or the belief that an individual's conscience trumps outside regulation in matters of moral decision-making. This might come as a surprise to some people, as the Catholic Church is not exactly known for its healthy distribution of power, but it is written in the official catechism. But the catechism doesn't leave it at that; it continues on to address the importance of *forming* one's conscience.

> The education of the conscience is a lifelong task. From the earliest years, it awakens the child to the knowledge and practice of the interior law recognized by conscience. Prudent education teaches virtue; it prevents or cures fear, selfishness and pride, resentment arising from guilt, and feelings of complacency, born of human weakness and faults. The education of the conscience guarantees freedom and engenders peace of heart.[8]

For our purposes in this chapter, I believe we can substitute the word "intuition" for the catechism's "conscience." We have a sacred obligation to mindfully and prayerfully form our intuition to line up with the guidance of Wisdom/Sophia, which means we must never cease to actively uproot fear, selfishness, pride, and other distractions. It means we seek out effective counseling to address wounds from our past. It means we educate ourselves on the experience of others, especially the marginalized and oppressed. It might mean we find a certified spiritual director to help us discern the movement of God in our life.

Forming our intuition is a lot of work, and there is no finish line. But as we walk the journey of becoming women who embody a spirituality of wholeness, we will find an ease to our stride and a spring in our step as we tread the path. Becoming intuitive women requires much from us, but the reward is that we can reclaim our voice as the mouthpiece of God. And as author Kathy Khang says, "Voice is not limited to what comes out of my mouth, but out of my being."[9]

May that which comes out of both your mouth and your being be the truest things you know.

— Going Deeper —

Carve out the time and space to spend in reflection, whether that is a long soak in a warm bath, taking a solitary walk, or getting cozy in a chair with a pen and journal. As you feel yourself relax and your breath deepen, put one hand on your gut and thank Wisdom/Sophia for the way she guides you.

Remember a time when you ignored your intuition and regretted it later. Then reflect on the following questions:

Why didn't I trust what I felt?

Who did I choose to listen to instead?

What would I like to let go of in order to move forward differently?

If you're honest, do you feel your voice is fully your own, or are you mostly answering from someone else's influence? How might it feel to reclaim your own voice? What is one actionable step you can take toward this right now?

Speak one or more of these affirmations aloud to yourself:

I am good, and I have good ideas.

I contain deep wisdom within me.

Wisdom/Sophia is always guiding me.

My children and my world need me to trust my intuition.

I trust myself.

PART / TWO

Flowing Outward

nine

Embodying Hospitality

Fertility That Embraces the Whole World

Having an older sister with whom I was very close, I was as prepared as anyone could be for the coming of my first period. I had witnessed Elise bleed monthly for several years, so I wasn't afraid of menstruation. But like many young girls I was ambivalent about the prospect, eager to enter into womanhood but pained at the idea of leaving childhood behind.

My first period arrived over Christmas break in seventh grade, and by divine grace it came at my grandmother Irene's house, where we had traveled for the holidays. Like millions of young women before me—and unlike so many in this day and age—I bled for the first time surrounded by the women in my family: in the home of a matriarch, attended to by my older sister and mother, under a roof that was crowded with aunts and female cousins. There were men present in the house too, of course, but I remember nothing of them that day. What I do remember is that I felt safe, cared for, and supported by a lineage of women I was proud to be included in.

Not every woman has fond memories of her first period; in fact, my story is more likely in the minority. But once upon a time it was different. Ages and ages ago, before monotheism, before patriarchy, back when, as Clarissa Pinkola Estés says, women ran with the wolves,[1] the menarche (or, first menstrual bleeding) of a girl was celebrated in lavish communal rituals. She was surrounded by other women. She was honored and exalted. She was recognized as a conduit of divine energy and seen as extremely powerful.[2]

Today one can still find similar rituals in indigenous communities around the globe as native peoples refuse to sacrifice the sacredness of femininity on the altar of modernity, but most of us in the modern West have been taught to dread the coming of our period. As girls, we were educated on our bodies in rushed presentations by our teachers or fumbling explanations by our mothers, who were given no better themselves. We were teased by other girls for starting "too early" or "too late" or for wearing the "wrong" kind of sanitary aid. We were accused of being "on the rag" by boys any time we refused to smile or spoke our mind or dissented from the majority opinion. Our blood was used against us. Our blood became our shame.

As women now, we are less self-conscious about bleeding and mostly just feel inconvenienced by it. We sigh at catching the first sight of blood for the three-hundredth time, calculating the annoyance of extra bathroom runs, uterine cramps, fatigue, and raging hormones in an already busy week. We are reminded by the medical community that there are birth control methods that can be used to prevent the process from happening entirely and some of us take them up on it, because why bother with the pain and the mess at all? No one has ever suggested to us that this spotting of blood in our underwear might be a visible sign of an invisible grace. How did we lose such a transformative perspective?

In her book *Women's Rites of Passage*, author and psychiatrist Abigail Brenner explains that in ancient pagan traditions, menstruation was held in high reverence by the entire community: men and women alike believed a woman was more powerful during her monthly bleeding. But "as this egalitarian society was replaced by a male-centered one, all things belonging to part of the sacred and hallowed feminine mystery came to be feared and diminished," Brenner writes. "Men created their own elaborate purification rituals for women, whom they now viewed as defiled and untouchable. . . . Menstruation was turned into an event surrounded by humiliation—and not just the first time, but over and over again through the course of a woman's life. . . . Eventually, women took this shame upon themselves, living out a false modesty and feeling that female physiological functions were somehow tainted."[3]

This may be painful for you to digest; it is for me. But we have to face the discomforting ways in which the male dominance among religions has resulted in shame surrounding the female body. In becoming spiritually mature persons, we are asked to integrate both the beauty and the failures of our religious traditions in order to learn from the past and move forward in becoming a community of greater wholeness. It doesn't mean we have to leave our faith traditions, but it does mean we have to push for awareness and appropriate change.

We can each be a part of bringing that change by treating the female body and menstruation with honor, whether it's our own, our daughters', or our friends'. We can choose our words and tone carefully. We can make menarche a ritual for the preteen girls in our lives. We can honor our bodies by getting extra rest and nourishment—both physical and spiritual—during our time of the month. We can create personal rituals surrounding our cycles that I'll delve into in the "Going Deeper" section at the end of this chapter. We can let our creativity, our *fertility*, run wild.

Because that's really what fertility is: the ability to create. I don't just mean the ability to create children. Some of the most creative women I know have never borne children, so the two can't possibly be mutually exclusive. The physical ability to bear life is not all that it means to be a generative woman.

If you've never spent time perusing ancient fertility statues, you need to check out a good book from the library and fill an entire afternoon on the couch flipping through the pages with a mug of tea in hand. Absorbing such empowering imagery has a profound effect on the psyche. Fertility statues come in all shapes and sizes, but many are sculpted into the bodies of women more voluptuous than we are accustomed to seeing represented. Lots of boulder-sized breasts abound. Proudly exposed vaginal canals are par for the course.

Scientists have found statues of fertility goddesses that date as far back as the Upper Paleolithic Period, or about forty thousand years ago. These cultures were neither shy about the female body nor hesitant to ascribe great power to it. Fertility statues were used to pray not only to receive the blessing of children but also for the fertility of the land—as well as a way to honor sex and love as an end in themselves.

Some might balk at viewing these pagan items, but the point isn't to worship them. Rather, examining them with curiosity and asking questions about what you can learn from your ancestors might produce more fruit in your soul that you would think. For us who are now living in an age of body-shaming and a culture that cannot handle the sight of a noneroticized vagina, there is something deeply healing about gazing on these sculptures and finding renewed reverence for the wonder that is our own flesh.

Our Natural Rhythms

It's no secret that our bodies are connected to the earth and its life cycles. Our monthly periods mirror the phases of the moon. Our bodies are gatekeepers of life. "Mother Earth" and "Mother Nature" are common nomenclature. Mythologies like that of Demeter and Persephone connect the seasons of the year to the heart and soul of a woman. But the interconnection goes further than most of us realize.

In *Theology of the Womb*, Christy Angelle Bauman points out that the lifespan of a woman's uterus mirrors the greater life cycle of creation: adolescing (the premenstrual years that mirror spring), reproducing (the menstruating and fertile years that mirror summer), and senescing (the menopausal years that mirror autumn).[4] We see this same cycle of growth, creation, and death in plant life, weather patterns, lunar cycles, and in our own human lifespan. I even see it in my Catholic tradition in the liturgical rhythm of Ordinary Time (growing), Advent (creating), and Lent (dying).

But it doesn't stop there. There is, of course, a cycle *within* the life cycle of a woman's uterus. Bauman writes, "A woman's body bears another cycle every twenty-eight days, and much like the twenty-four hours from sunrise to sunrise tells us a story of creation, the uterus tells a story monthly through the female cycle. . . . God designed the uterus to convey God's image as Creator. This organ tells us a story in its life, in the cycles it undergoes every month. The female uterus is the part of the body that illustrates the *imago Dei* through the process of creating."[5]

Our menstrual cycles are so much more than merely the week of our blood. There is a rhythm and a wisdom to the mystery. In *Body Full of Stars*, Molly Caro May says that in our preovulation days, we are active and project-focused. During ovulation, we are fully enlivened and sensual. In the premenstrual time that has garnered such a negative reputation, women become discerning and brutally honest. May says this is not a time to make decisions or take new action; rather, this is a time to gather valuable information. Then when our bleeding begins, we enter a time of inner reflection and spiritual connection. And the cycle begins again.[6]

May invites women to refuse the temptation to shame ourselves for our tendency to change from week to week; sometimes we are level-headed and calm, other times we are a geyser of emotion. "Inconsistency is how we are made," she writes. "We are *of* the moon, and the moon does not present one way all the time."[7]

Magical, isn't it?

Magical, aren't you?

But I can't speak of the uterus without acknowledging there is pain associated with it. Few of us live in lifelong peace with our fertility; it seems to always be either over- or underperforming—or else it's the source of omnipresent questions we're unsure how to answer. *Will we get pregnant before we're ready? What if we never manage to get pregnant? Should we have another baby? How will we know when we're "done"? How much health risk is too much? How do we grieve the babies we've lost and hold the ones we have? How do we space our babies? What if we can't? What fertility assistance are we comfortable with, and what is outside our conscience?* The struggle with our fertility is part of what it means to be human.

To have a healthy relationship with our fertility we have to stop seeing it as being solely about birthing babies; whether or not we bear children, and long after we stop, women's bodies bear the physical evidence of a procreative God.

So how do we embrace a fertility that goes deeper than our role as mother and into the earth-nurturing, life-giving, art-making parts of us that aren't usually defined as fertility but are exactly that? What would it look like to procreate the divine into the world in ways presently hidden from our sight?

Accepting Disappointment

A few years ago, Eric and I, with our three children at the time, tried to start a house of hospitality in the Catholic Worker tradition, which hinges on the works of mercy, dignified living for those in homelessness, and solidarity with the poor. We had once been part of a vibrant Catholic Worker community that was now floundering, and we longed to return and raise our kids in the atmosphere of mercy and justice we'd encountered there.

The effort required us to move out of state, find new jobs, reconnect with old friends, and live in voluntary poverty: in short, it required everything. And we tried to give just that for one long hot summer, coming up against an unjust landlord, the loss of running water, no medication for one child as we waited for Medicaid, another child's anxiety, no clear employment path for Eric, and, oh yes, a surprise pregnancy.

Ever feel like the universe is trying to tell you something?

Pioneering that house of hospitality didn't work out for us. After three months we moved back to the town we'd left, Eric resumed his old job, and we made our peace with a life of small faithfulness to the hope of social justice. It was the right decision for our family, but one that surfaced every grief I had choked down in my adult life—a life that so badly wanted to impact the world but just kept getting more flattened with every attempt to do so.

For weeks I mourned the death of a dream I had wanted dearly, all the while struggling to embrace the new baby growing inside me that served as a physical reminder of the limitations of family life. I loved my children, yet with each one's arrival, I had smaller reserves to offer anything to the rest of the world I also loved.

How hard it can sometimes be to welcome a child. Even though you know you're going to love them; even though you know you will lose yourself in their tiny fingers and searching mouths the very moment you meet them; even though you know that one sticky grin at three or bear hug at seventeen will completely undo you—even though you know these things, it can be painfully hard to welcome a child as you watch the life you once knew change right before your eyes.

How much harder for those among us who have been asked to welcome a child for too short a time: those who have bled when they shouldn't, those who labored but whose arms remained empty, those who have seen tubes attached to their children in hospital beds, those women among us who couldn't keep the one thing in the world they would have given everything for. How hard it would it be to welcome a child for a moment when what you wanted was to hold them for eternity.

We don't get to choose what kind of welcome we will be asked to extend, whether it will be brief or long, straightforward or complex, biological or adoptive. Making peace with our fertility means accepting the fear and pain of what it is to be human—of what it is to love. It means recognizing that Spirit cannot be contained by clenched fists; it will always have a way of slipping between our helpless fingers, pulling us in close, and whispering gently into our ears, *All shall be well.*

Extending Hospitality to Our Children

If there is anything I've learned from birthing four babies in five years—only half of whom were planned—it's that welcoming our children does not always come as instinctively as we once assumed it would. And I don't just mean their births; I also mean the day-in and day-out interruption, inconvenience, changed plans, and disrupted productivity. When we engage in the mundane rhythms of attending to the needs of our children throughout their lifespan, we are choosing to welcome them all over again, dozens of times every day.

When our family had to fold our cards on the house of hospitality and I was deep in grief, it comforted me to know that Dorothy Day, cofounder of the Catholic Worker movement, had expressed to her only daughter, Tamar—a mother of ten!—that

Tamar's was a house of hospitality too, albeit of a different nature. If such a radical icon of social justice could look at motherhood and rename it hospitality, I knew there was something I was missing. Having children seemed to have pulled me further from the hope of being a transforming force in the world, but somehow that didn't feel like the end of the story. Was there something God was doing in me through motherhood that could uniquely shape me into a woman who would actually have more to bring to the social landscape, not less?

In welcoming children we learn to welcome the stranger, a command explicitly written in the sacred texts of the Torah, Bible, Qur'an, and Upanishads; in fact, the call to show hospitality to outsiders is one of the most unifying elements of the major world religions. Seeing this, we must realize the importance of the choice, not just for the state of the world but equally for the state of our souls. If most ancient religious traditions are to be trusted, it would seem that we have a choice: welcome the stranger and open ourselves to the movement of God, or refuse and lose the opportunity for inner growth.

Perhaps this is what Jesus knew when he said, "Whoever welcomes one such child in my name welcomes me" (Matt. 18:5). Sure, there is a mystical quality of finding Christ in everyone you meet, especially those with the least amount of power and social capital; but I wonder too if Jesus knew that welcoming children would work the muscle of hospitality in those of us who would otherwise remain unmalleable and hard-hearted.

When we welcome a child, we exercise the muscle of radical hospitality. As the muscle grows stronger, we expand. Not automatically—it's not a magical side effect of parenthood. But if we are living attentive to the Spirit within us and seeking to be transformed into more loving and compassionate human beings, then mothering little ones can give us a substantial head start.

When we welcome a child, we practice the virtue of stopping for the one in need, the practice that Jesus called us to when he said a good shepherd leaves ninety-nine sheep to find the one who is lost. Babies and young children naturally cause our worlds to stop their rotations and find new revolutions around these little ones. Their needs dictate how much we sleep, when we eat, how we make decisions, and what we do in our spare time. Once you invite a child into your heart, you've given them a preferential place there for the rest of their lives. Through welcoming children, we practice the commitment to walk with another human being for the long haul.

When we welcome a child, we practice a "people first" lifestyle. When we foster a teenager, we are declaring that his right to a family is more important than our right to unencumbered freedom. When we give birth to yet another baby, we are saying her life is more valuable than a bigger house or a newer car. When we welcome children, we work the muscle of prioritizing human beings over material goods, schedules, achievements, or wealth.

Motherhood teaches us the radical generosity of offering what we can for another. And if we are responsive to the expansion within us, then slowly—often quite unexpectedly—we find that the boundary lines of what constitutes family widen.

At one point in her book *Braiding Sweetgrass*, Native American author and environmental scientist Robin Wall Kimmerer describes her decades-long commitment to restoring the pond that falls within the property lines of her land. Initially motivated by her young daughters' desire for a place to swim and her own desire to give them everything as a newly single mother, Kimmerer undertook the slow work of restoration. As the years ticked by and the girls aged into young women, it became clear that her window of opportunity was closing. Eventually she realized her daughters would never swim in the pond. But Kimmerer knows there is more to the story. She writes,

> So it is my grandchildren who will swim in this pond, and others whom the years will bring. The circle of care grows larger

and caregiving for my little pond spills over to caregiving for other waters. The outlet from my pond runs downhill to my good neighbor's pond. What I do here matters. Everybody lives downstream. . . . I have shed tears into that flow when I thought that motherhood would end. But the pond has shown me that being a good mother doesn't end with creating a home where just my children can flourish. A good mother grows into a richly eutrophic old woman, knowing that her work doesn't end until she creates a home where all of life's beings can flourish.[8]

Extending Hospitality to Everyone

According to scholar Cynthia Bourgeault, we've done a poor job of interpreting Jesus's teaching in Matthew 19:19 about loving our neighbor. Jesus's point is not to compel us to love our neighbor *as much as* ourselves, but to love them *as an extension* of ourselves. She writes,

> It's just "Love your neighbor as yourself"—as a continuation of your very own being. It's a complete seeing that your neighbor is you. There are not two individuals out there, one seeking to better herself at the price of the other, or to extend charity to the other; there are simply two cells of the one great Life. . . . And as these two cells flow into one another, experiencing that one Life from the inside, they discover that "laying down one's life for another" is not a loss of one's self but a vast expansion of it.[9]

Laying down my life for my children, when done out of healthy self-giving rather than dutiful obligation, is not, as Bourgeault asserts, a loss of self but a vast expansion of it. My small, infantile brain gets to grasp what it means to be interconnected to my fellow human. That concept is too mystical to comprehend on a large scale, but mothering my babies teaches it to me in small pieces, one on one. I belong to them and they belong to me.

But the mystery of motherhood is that it will never stop there. When rooted in God, the maternal will always expand. It is in its very nature to do so. True feminine fertility pushes us past the boundaries of DNA and unveils the mystical reality that all the world is our child. The fibers of motherhood weave together to create a tapestry large enough to envelop, nurture, and defend every soul we meet.

On May 25, 2020, an unarmed black man named George Floyd was suffocated under the knee of a police officer in Minneapolis. As he struggled for breath for eight minutes and forty-six seconds, as onlookers videotaped the scene and pleaded with the officer to stop, Floyd called out for his mother. And then he took his last breath.

For months, Americans far and wide took to the streets of their neighborhoods and cities to protest Floyd's murder, creating the greatest civil rights movement in the US since the March on Washington. In city after city, protest after protest, there were women of every race holding up signs that said, "All mothers were summoned when George Floyd called out for his mama." The maternal spirit had been awakened.

If we are doing motherhood right, it *will* crack us open. And when we begin to translate our love for our children into love for the strangers around us, we begin to walk out the holistic meaning of fertility. We begin to create and birth love wherever we go.

This is the power of motherhood. The power of fertility. The power of hospitality. The power of the blood of a woman.

— Going Deeper —

If you are currently having regular periods, mark the calendar for your next menstrual week and plan ahead for entering into the time mindfully. This might mean scheduling a massage, blocking off nights to take a hot bath, letting your family know you'll be sleeping in, buying some scented candles, or ordering a spiritually empowering book to have on hand. When your period comes, spend one late night praying alone under the light of the moon.

Consider the ancient belief that women were more powerful when menstruating—closer to a God who is always fertile. What if that were true? What then would you want to try during this time? Creating art? Longer prayer and meditation? Writing a letter of protest? Taking political or social action? Applying for a new job? Perhaps if you take a leap of faith, the power of God will overtake you.

If you are not currently having regular periods for any reason, you can do the same thing by blocking off a Saturday or entire weekend to do the aforementioned actions as a time of focused honor of your body and fertility. Create some space to process your feelings about your relationship with your fertility: where that relationship has been, as well as where you'd like it to be in the future. Name and honor the parts of yourself that are procreating love in other ways too.

ten

Becoming Gentle

Tenderness in Exchange for Criticism

I sat across from my son, whose little body trembled with rage, and searched my brain for what to say. Just moments before, he had yelled the f-word at his brother in the midst of an argument. Yes, *that* f-word.

Am I a total failure as a parent? I wondered. *Who deals with this at this age?* My own parents certainly didn't. My embarrassment and anger simmered just below the surface, urging me to verbally clobber him with a lecture on respect, appropriate language, and what the long list of his consequences would be. *But his eyes.*

His eyes told me he was in pain—pain that went far beyond a sibling scuffle and into a place he didn't know how to touch. He cried through his rage, and I saw the raw wound of grief. I sighed. My top-notch mom lecture would have to take a back seat this time. "Come here, honey." I drew him in close.

What followed was the most honest, heartfelt conversation we had ever shared. He was able to name specific pain that he had never spoken before, and I held him and affirmed its validity. With every sentence that passed across his lips, his sense of safety deepened and gave him permission to further express the abyss of his grief. I didn't do much but acknowledge his heartache and tell him how sorry I was for the load he carried inside. It was enough.

It's no exaggeration to say that moment, that decision of mine, was a crucial one in my son's life. It broke through a barrier he had erected in his heart that told him his full self was not safe to come out, that his hurts and fears would be too much for his family to handle. Now don't get me wrong; there have been plenty of times before and after that he has been subjected to lectures and consequences. That's a part of life and a part of parenting. But on this day, we reached an unspoken agreement with each other that his heart would always be accounted for and that he would never be judged on actions alone.

This is one of my proudest parenting moments to date. You surely have yours as well: those times when you were able to cut through the behaviors and the noise and address the root issue of the heart. These are the moments when we feel best about our motherhood—the moments when we look at ourselves and feel that we're doing a pretty good job at this parenting thing after all.

Conversely, the times I feel worst about myself as a mom are the times when I am callous and don't stop to see my child, the times when I am overly critical or lose my temper. I imagine the same is true for you. Noticing these things—noticing the times when we feel good about our parenting and the times when we don't—calls us to ask questions about the way we want to parent, the factors that contribute to our ability to be good parents, and the practical tools for moving forward.

But this information is not relegated to parenting alone: it tells us something about the human heart. As is so often the case in motherhood, what happens on a micro level with our children holds up a mirror to the macro level of the human race. The human heart flourishes under gentleness and withers under criticism.

Forming Connections

Our family has been deeply formed by the work of the late Dr. Karyn Purvis of the Institute of Child Development at Texas Christian University. The research and teachings of Purvis, and those whom she trained, are primarily responsible for our departure from an obedience-based parenting mentality to a connection-based one. Purvis developed the Trust Based Relationship Intervention model for parents, caregivers, and teachers of children who have been through trauma. But what I appreciate so much about Purvis's work and legacy is that the implications do not end with at-risk children, or even children in general, but rather extend to all of humanity and our most primal desires for belonging and trust.

"When you connect to the heart of a child, everything is possible," Purvis writes.[1] Notice her word choice: not *guide* or *correct* or *train* the heart of a child, but *connect*. The human heart is wired to reach for deep, authentic connection; once we experience it, our brains receive the message that it is safe to settle in, think rationally, and make wise decisions. The principle is just as important to acknowledge in relation to ourselves as it is in relation to our children. We all need connection, both externally with others and internally within ourselves.

Most of us have our fair share of mom guilt. "I never thought I'd be a mom who yells," I've heard many women bemoan. "I never expected to be so . . . mean!" another friend of mine confessed, and I nodded right along with her. Parenting is incredibly hard work, and frankly it's just impossible for a human being to get it right every time. We will make mistakes. We will mess up. But what I learned from Purvis is that it's not a matter of *whether* we will break connection with our kids—we will—but a matter of how we reconnect with them. This is true whether our child is two or twenty-two.

Here are some examples of guiding questions for this type of connection work:

- Do we get on their eye level and take ownership for what we did wrong, or do we abandon the topic and leave it unaddressed and festering?
- Do we seek to understand the heart issue behind the behaviors—our own as well as theirs—or do we leave it at surface level?
- Do we make an effort to regain trust by doing it better next time, or do we perpetuate the same cycles all over again, leaving our apologies feeling empty and valueless?
- If we are stuck in cycles, do we seek out counseling or other tools to help us break free from them?

The parent-child relationship is a magnified experience of the human-human relationship. We are offered the possibility of becoming gentler, happier, more compassionate people by participating in a crash course every day. The way we practice interacting with our kids is in some nuanced sense the way we interact with everyone else, and—maybe most surprisingly of all—the way we interact with ourselves.

In the past few years I have heard more therapist friends speak of "reparenting your inner child." This doesn't mean your own parents were by default abusive, neglectful, or otherwise failed miserably (although that is tragically a part of some of our stories); it means they and you were imperfect humans living in an imperfect world, and there are wounds we all carry into adulthood that can disrupt our becoming more whole—unless we learn what to do with them.

My friend Aundi Kolber is one voice I trust as I learn about the concept of reparenting the little girl inside of me. As a therapist and as someone who has done much of her own inner work, she explains that our inner child "lives" in the part of the brain called the amygdala, which tends to run amok in stressful situations, whether or not we realize it's happening. Aundi says that learning to pay compassionate attention to yourself is a huge part of the work of reparenting your inner child. She writes, "This work is stewarding toward ourselves the love and compassion that God feels toward us. This practice can help us find the middle place where we allow the wounds of our younger selves to be validated without being controlled by them."[2] Aundi calls this "trying softer," and that terminology has resonated with tens of thousands of people.

Our parenting tends to hold up a mirror to our deepest, often unacknowledged, beliefs about ourselves. The way we treat ourselves will always shape the way we treat our children. If we are highly self-critical, we will also be critical of them. If we ignore or downplay our own needs, we will diminish the validity of theirs. If we don't stop to reparent the scared or injured feelings of our inner child, we won't be able to access the deepest feelings of our children. As much as we would like to think we can parent our kids well without doing our own inner work, we're mistaken. Everything is connected.

Recognizing Our Weaknesses

We pass on our patterns of functioning, even the nonverbal ones, to our children—sometimes because they are watching us intently and sometimes because they learn by osmosis. Scientific studies are revealing more clearly than ever that our physical bodies store information that is passed down from generation to generation. African American communities address this when they speak of generational trauma borne out over and over again in their families—even so many years after slavery. Our bodies tell the stories of our families.

Quantum physicists now know that rather than being a solid mass, our bodies consist of many particles that are always in motion, each interrelating and connecting us in undetectable ways with one another and with other living organisms. If this is true for living things in general, how much more true is it of a parent-child relationship?

I would hope that your love for yourself would be enough to motivate you to tend to the hurting places inside of you, but if it feels too easy to disregard your own well-being, consider the fact that looking inward and extending compassion to yourself really does benefit your children too. They need a mother who is gentle with herself. No matter how kind you are to *them*, they will struggle to grow to fully love themselves if they do not see self-love modeled.

This is where you might be tempted to assess how you have fallen short and then slide down the slope of despair and never look back, but please don't. You have not screwed up your kids. You have done a lot of things right and a few things wrong, and there is an open space before you to grow. No matter how old you are, no matter how old your children are, there is always time to do better. There is time to reparent your own inner child. There is time to reparent your children. There is time to choose tenderness and let the fruits of that choice unfold. Don't give way to a self-critical spirit.

For some reason we humans have internalized the belief that self-criticism actually does something. It's almost as though by punishing ourselves for not getting it right we feel we are making up for whatever error we committed. Of course, we're not making up for anything at all. Our self-beratement accomplishes nothing but wasting our energy and making us think less of ourselves.

In her book *Boundless Compassion*, Joyce Rupp writes, "When we become absorbed in nasty judgments and treat our limitations as an enemy, our energy escapes into a war with self. Consequently, we lose life-giving, growthful openness to the Holy One's transformative love. It is an illusion to think we can get rid of everything we do not like or want to have in our personality. We *can* learn, however, not to let these parts have power over us, not to act on them."[3] Reiterating the same message, American Buddhist nun Pema Chödrön says, "Repressing your tendencies, shaming yourself, calling yourself bad—these will never help you realize transformation."[4]

Both women mention transformation, and that really is what we seek, isn't it? But when we don't know how to reach for it or how to attain it, we settle for putting ourselves down instead. After all, spewing out something to fill the silence is easier than asking what the silence might require of us.

Forging a New Path

I happen to not have a perfectionistic personality type; I could probably afford to be a little *more* self-critical. But women like me need the message of gentleness with self as much as the type A women of the world do; it might just look a little different.

I truly love being a mother. It has not been an easy road, having five kids in nine years, and at the onset I had no idea how much I would learn about myself through the journey or how difficult it would prove to be. But I do adore my little people, which is why the biggest red flag I have learned to heed is when that feeling of warmth and enjoyment starts to wane.

When I find myself more annoyed with my children than delighted by them, or my temper flies off the handle day after day, or when I am convinced I will go stark raving mad if asked to prepare one more godforsaken meal, I can now identify that something needs to change. Because I know I love my children, because I know I am generally a kind and competent parent, I can recognize that when I am not my best self for an extended length of time I need to start looking at what to do differently around here.

Do you know the adage about the definition of insanity—doing the same thing over and over and expecting different results? This is the trap that snares mothers everywhere. The labor that we're doing is hard, no doubt about it. But instead of considering how it might feel a bit easier we tend to just put our heads down and keep doing what we think must be done. Perhaps this is why we have created a subculture that normalizes things like wine or coffee as the unifying sustenance that keeps mothers everywhere afloat. Call me a dreamer, but I think women deserve better.

When we are not doing well, it's not a potentially addictive substance that we need. We need change. It might be a simple change like an hour of alone time in the mornings or scheduling an appointment with a counselor, or it might be a major change like reentering the workforce. But one of the most important ways we practice tenderness with self is to notice what isn't working and address it.

This has been a big area of growth in my life. I am the kind of person who will continue to do the same thing over and over and expect a different result—or at least complain about getting the same result a hundred times. I'm a grit-your-teeth, dig-in-your-heels, just-keep-trucking kind of gal. In fact, I used to take pride in that. I thought it made me a strong woman. I was wrong.

My "keep on keeping on" motto wasn't making me strong; it was separating part of my soul from me. It was stuffing down every valid need I had until I'd become nothing. It was making me too grouchy to enjoy my children and too resentful to enjoy my lover. And it all came tumbling down when I began asking, "What if . . . ?"

*What if I was allowed to make big changes and our family
didn't fall apart?*

*What if I listened to my own heart the way I said I wanted
to listen to my children's hearts?*

What if I became gentle with myself instead of forceful?

What if I believed my needs were legitimate?

Giving myself permission to explore these kinds of questions
freed me to imagine a better life for myself and, by extension,
a better life for my children; a life in which their mom could be
happier, more playful, and more tender with them—because
she'd finally become tender with herself.

— Going Deeper —

Avid hikers are familiar with the idea of cairns—that is, stacked
rocks sporadically placed along the trail. While the stacked
rocks are visually appealing, the intention of the little structure is to confirm to hikers that they are on the right track.
Today I invite you to create a cairn as your own monument to
gentleness.

Step outside and gather five or so stones. (The flatter the
better for stacking, but do what you can.) On a shelf or win-
dowsill or other appropriate place, stack the stones one by one
to create a little cairn.

Take a moment to study the stack. More than likely, it is
imperfect. Perhaps it leans to the side or consists of drastically
different kinds of rocks. Allow yourself to appreciate this im-
perfection; be generous in your thoughts about it. Resist the
urge to criticize what you have made. Let the stack of rocks
serve as a reminder that as you seek gentleness with yourself
and others, you are on the right path.

eleven

Releasing Control
Permission to Stop Playing God

I remember well the days of waking up in the mornings and immediately darting to the computer in hopes of seeing an email with good news about our adoption. Bringing our son Alyosha home consumed my mind nearly every waking minute. Lucky for me, this was before the era of the smartphone; otherwise, I doubtless would have developed some legitimate form of obsessive disorder. As it was, depression was my lone companion.

They say hindsight is 20/20, and, looking back, it's almost cute how I thought our adoption process was excruciating. Now I can see it was relatively smooth and quite timely, as far as those things go. But experience has a lot to do with expectation, and I was not prepared to relinquish control of the timeline in my head. Every day that I waited for my boy felt like a century, and even the tiniest bump in the road found me crumpled in a heap on the floor. I held on like my life depended on it, even though it was almost entirely out of my hands.

I clung to the desire for control as though by doing so I could determine my son's fate, as though I could keep him safe half a world away, as though I could keep Eric's anxiety at bay and my marriage stable. If it could all just go according to my plan, I reasoned, everything would end up as it should be.

I was young then and not yet a mother. I had the luxury of believing in the illusion of control. But holding Alyosha for the first time, and then embarking on the journey of parenting him, swept that illusion away like dust, particle by particle. Suddenly I was a mother, thrown into an abyss of love and fear and the truth that control is beyond my reach. The dismantling has never relented, no not once, but still I find myself clamoring to hold tighter anyway.

My boy is a preteen now, black as the night and tender as the soil, and if I could just be in charge of his life—if I could be god for him always—then my fears would subside. At least I like to think this is true. I know it's a lie; I know it's the great delusion of motherhood back at it again. When he was a baby, I longed to control social workers and court orders and orphanage nannies and emails; now his limbs lengthen and his voice will soon change, and what I want to control these days are police officers and middle-school peers and racist bigots that don't deserve to kiss the ground his precious feet walk on.

But I control nothing of the sort. I never have.

Parenting from Fear

As moms, we would do nearly anything to keep our kids safe, healthy, and happy; maternal love is one of the most motivating forces in the world. When our children are infants, we want to control their sleep patterns and developmental timelines. When they are in school, we want to control their friend groups and social interests. When they are adults, we want to control where they live and who they marry. And for each one of these wantings there are thousands in between. To love is to will someone else's good, but we tend to believe only *we* know what that good might be.

In *Daybook*, Anne Truitt's acclaimed diary, the artist observes, "Generosity is often the stalking horse of control."[1] Isn't this to some degree every woman's truth? Perhaps especially a mother's? We bend over backward to come to the rescue—because we want the outcome to be as we see fit. We trample our own boundaries and exhaust ourselves "helping" those we love—because we don't trust what might happen if we decline to do so. And we exist within a society that lauds such "generosity" as a great moral good, so our dysfunction continues to be rewarded from the outside, even if it is ultimately harmful to our children, partners, or those with whom we live in community.

It's painful to confront the idea that the help we offer might not be as altruistic as we'd like to believe. It's even more painful to question whether our generosity might be keeping our loved ones from their own growth. What we gain in security in the short term might cost them grief and harm in the long run.

Early childhood educator Maria Montessori was known to urge parents and teachers never to do for a child what they could do for themselves. The advice is enlightening when the context is a three-year-old pouring their own cup of milk; it's agonizing when it's a sixteen-year-old choosing where to apply for college. But at every age and stage, we have to dig deep within ourselves and find the inner freedom to let that proverbial caterpillar become a butterfly. If we fail to release our grip, we do our children a disservice.

The desire to control is birthed in love, yes, but it's also birthed in fear. Mothering our children is not the only place our control manifests itself, not even close. But it's often the most obvious, the place we're most acutely aware of it. Our struggle with seeking to control our kids is usually a good indicator of how much control we are trying to exert in other spheres of our lives too, and how little we are trusting God.

Because we know this is ultimately what it's about, don't we? Trust. In theory we want to entrust our loved ones to divine love, but in practice it gets blurry. I am told to "let go and let God," but how do I let go seven hundred times every day of my life? This is a long road, yet it's not one without hope. There is freedom to be had.

Understanding Our Desire for Control

But before we can release our grip on needing control, we have to reckon with the roots of our relationship to it. While the desire for control is a universally human trait, it seems to be a more pronounced interior battle for women. There is a reason stereotypes like the "helicopter mom" exist, a reason words like *suffocating* and *manipulative* are more often applied to women than men, a reason we are the butt of sour marital jokes about "the old ball and chain." Why is our desire for control so obvious that it has become stereotyped? Could it be that it is rooted in repressed feelings of powerlessness?

Some of us may recall this scene from *My Big Fat Greek Wedding*: the main character, thirty-year-old Toula, is crying on her mother's shoulder because her father refuses to allow her to enroll in college classes. Toula's charming Greek mother assures her that she can change his mind, because "the man is the head [of the house], but the woman is the neck and she can turn the head any way she wants."[2]

I wonder if the screenwriter anticipated the overwhelming reception of that now iconic line, how many women would recite it to one another in winks and knowing giggles, how mothers and daughters of all ages and races would see their own experience reflected back to them from the screen. That line has been immortalized in the Hollywood canon because it gives voice to both the universal grief of the subordinate female position and the ingenuity of women to hold power in whatever way they can.

Seeking control when one lacks equal power often manifests as manipulation, and if we're honest we see this in ourselves all too well. It's one thing to chuckle at Toula's charismatic mother; it's another to admit how the longing for agency morphs into manipulation in our own behaviors.

The social structures of our homes, workforce, governments, and religious institutions have intentionally (not accidentally) been set up to deny equal power to women. This is slowly improving, but it doesn't change the fact that imbalanced conditions are in place and will take a long time to equalize. Given this reality, is it any wonder that women throughout the ages have sought more subtle ways to grasp at controlling whatever we possibly can?

Science confirms that it's actually the most capable women, not the least, who do this. A 2015 study conducted by the University of Plymouth found that young women with high emotional intelligence were more likely to engage in manipulative behaviors.[3] This is heartbreaking evidence that the most astute among us are interpreting our surroundings as hostile to our authentic input. We intuit a lack of agency even as teens, so we become passive-aggressive and do what we can to best survive the environment we find ourselves in.

This is not a defense of manipulation; it's unhealthy and produces rotten fruit in all parties involved. But to get free from the habit that haunts so many of our relationships, we have to get to the root of why we subconsciously decided somewhere along the way that manipulation was our best bet. Why did that feel like the only power we would ever have?

Are you cringing at the word *power*? If so, it's not surprising. In the secular world, the unapologetic desire for power is a faux pas; in the world of religion and faith, it's downright sinful.

Love does not grasp for power, we are assured. Love seeks only to serve. Love goes low in humility.

These were the answers I heard from a well-known priest when he was asked in a video interview about the lack of opportunity for women in the Catholic Church. True power is not about position but about service, he demurred, and the beauty of Christianity is that anyone can serve. Mmm-kay. But the people with the penises have a whole lot more options for *how* to serve than the people with the vaginas. Are we really going to keep pretending there's no imbalance there?

In religious traditions that have predominantly been formed and led by men (and, if you're counting, that's basically all of them), teachings about humility, servanthood, and sacrifice tend to be highly visible core components. These are noble virtues, but when left radically imbalanced they can be dangerous to the human psyche.

As a woman with a bent toward self-betrayal, the emphasis on these things has done no favors for my spiritual life. Over the years, as I have begun to identify the overwhelming messages of denying one's self that I've internalized in my experiences within the Christian church, I have been awakened to the damaging effects of these messages on my emotional and spiritual health. Like many women, the spiritual principles I personally needed reiterated were those reminding me of my own God-given agency and voice. Sadly, these have been few and far between.

It makes sense that male-led religious institutions would gravitate toward messages of self-sacrifice; messages like this help balance the scales to create healthier men in a world where every other social sphere encourages them toward individualism, personal achievement, and a bolstered sense of self. White men in particular have historically had the most power, the most opportunity, and the most wealth of any demographic in the world; and so it is entirely appropriate that an emphasis on deference to the other is exactly what they need to hear. It fills a necessary void for men and can serve to create a whole and healthy male consciousness.

And yet for women, these messages painfully tip the scales that were already off-center. Women have historically been the caregivers of children and the elderly; we are the ones to gestate, birth, and nurse babies. Self-deference and sacrifice come with the territory of being a woman, thanks to a combination of biology, evolution, and social conditioning. Many of us would say our lives are marked by the necessity of putting others before ourselves; that doesn't mean we always do it, but it does mean we tend to feel guilty when we don't.

Men, on the other hand, have historically been less immediately bound by the needs of others. In no way does that diminish the sincerity of their love; it is simply a different biological and social dynamic. Women's bodies require us to physically put babies' needs above our own convenience or comfort, and that experience—especially when layered generation upon generation—is just not something that can be embodied by men, who historically have worked or hunted independent from the family unit.

It is crucial that we recognize this discrepancy and name it. There is nothing wrong with you, woman. You are not a wretchedly selfish creature. You are simply existing within a moral system designed with someone else's life experience in mind. I don't believe that the men who uphold these messages are purposefully harming women, but I do believe they are painfully oblivious to their blind spots. They need women in positions of equal power to bring the balance that half the church desperately needs—in this and so many other ways.

It's time for women to quit being afraid to ask for power, and certainly time to refuse to be shamed for our desire for equality. The pursuit for equal power is not for the sake of power itself, as the misguided priest in the interview suggested, but for the sake of creating a more whole, just, and righteous world for *everyone*—which simply cannot happen if not everyone is represented where decisions are being made.

Letting Go of the Need for Control

"Hey mom, I have a joke!"

"Ok, buddy, hit me."

"How do you eat an elephant?"

(I've known this joke for thirty years but must pretend to have never heard it before.) "Hmm, I don't know. How do you eat an elephant?"

"One bite at a time! Haha!"

Addressing massive systemic inequalities is a daunting task, but this is how we do it. We pull out our dinner fork and our steak knife, and we take down that sucker one bite at a time. We advocate for shared power in our marriages, families, worship communities, and governments at every level. We stop accepting unequal representation. We believe our voices and perspectives are important and necessary in and of themselves, not as echo chambers of the status quo. And the more we feel our sense of agency restored, the healthier our relationship to control can become; because when we have power, there is no need to contrive sneaky ways to grab it.

But achieving shared power in relational and institutional spaces is not a magical cure for our ailment of clinging to control. If we are to live in true internal freedom, and invite others into that freedom as well, the exercise of letting go must become a spiritual practice. This means we devote time and attention to this heart issue rather than erring on the side of either repression or projection. As much as systems do need to change, no amount of external change can ultimately change our hearts—that's on us.

I am a practitioner of Ignatian spirituality in large part because of its emphasis on detachment. I need the daily reminder to release my grip on controlling outcomes and people. Every day, or at least most days, I take an internal assessment of my desires, frustrations, and emotional responses. I conscientiously decide to live in openness to the movement of the Spirit, recognizing that I don't have the full picture and—contrary to what I like to think—don't necessarily know what's best for another person or even for myself.

Curiosity about the principle of detachment has led me to the teachings of other religions as well, and one piece of wisdom that has lodged itself in my brain is a Taoist story of a farmer that dates two thousand years back. First the farmer's horse runs away, and his neighbors grieve his loss. Then the horse returns with twelve more horses, and the neighbors marvel at the farmer's luck. The farmer's son breaks his leg while taming one of the new horses, and the neighbors are beside themselves over the misfortune. But when the son is excused from going to war because he has a broken leg, his neighbors celebrate. At every plot twist, while his neighbors vacillate between mourning and rejoicing, the farmer himself refrains. With each new development he simply says, "Who knows what is truly bad and truly good?" Now that is some serious Ignatian detachment.

Detachment doesn't mean we choose not to care or are somehow not emotionally affected; it means we accept that some things are out of our control and that there is a cosmic wisdom much greater than our own. While it is right and good to do everything in our power to give our loved ones and ourselves the healthiest, most loving state of being that we can, our power only goes so far. They need to be free. They need *us* to be free.

In the end, there is no shortcut to showing up for life. Any journey is risky. It is risky for our children to have their own journeys, walking largely without us physically beside them. It is risky to not be in singular control of our marriages, winding our way with another entirely autonomous person. Being a human fully alive, and letting the humans we love be fully alive, is one of the bravest things we will ever do.

When we offer help, may it not have its roots in the desire for control. When we practice generosity, may it carry no ulterior motive or attachment to a specific outcome. May we refrain from offering our presence as a tool of control, but rather offering it as a tool to invite others to find themselves more authentically. And may we never give to another if it costs something too deep within ourselves. For true generosity is love, and love wills for all to be free—yes, even you.

— Going Deeper —

In Ignatian spirituality, the Examen is a five-part prayer meant to be prayed at the end of each day as a way to reflect on how we experienced God that day, as well as the ways we resisted divine movement. Before you go to bed tonight, try praying through the following steps of the Examen and notice whether you feel more inner freedom afterward:

1. *Become aware of God's presence.* Light a candle if you'd like. Inhale deeply and exhale slowly. Still your soul to sit simply and without an agenda before God, free of expectations.
2. *Review the day with gratitude.* Looking back on the course of the day, find a few things that spark gratitude within you. Offer that feeling back to God.
3. *Pay attention to your emotions.* Hone in on one or two encounters from the day, and let yourself become aware of the emotions that were stirred in you at the time—and that perhaps are stirring again as you reflect. Your emotions are neither positive nor negative; they are

simply information. What do you learn by observing these emotions? What would inner freedom look like in these places?

4. *Choose one feature of the day and pray from it.* Whether it be an interaction with a specific person or an interior battle within yourself, choose an element that stands out in your reflection on the day. Imagine the outcome or resolve that you have been hoping to see. Now open your hands, breathe, and release your hold on that outcome.

5. *Look toward tomorrow.* Take a moment to think about the day ahead. Where will you need to rely on God's presence? Where will you be tempted to seize control? Set an intention of detachment and ask for a greater awareness of the Spirit in those times.

twelve

Valuing Work

Spiritual Teachings of Household Labor

I have long had a nebulous relationship with housework. My own parents, though egalitarian in many ways, are Southern folks whose division of labor has always reflected the social code of the time and place in which they were raised. My mother and maternal grandmother both had professional careers outside the home—Maw Maw was a bit of a marvel in the 1950s and '60s—but both women also exclusively saw to the cooking, cleaning, and laundering chores. My father's mother rose before dawn to work a full-time factory job so they could make ends meet, and she returned home at the end of the day to singlehandedly manage the household chores of a family of five. Mississippi men just did not cook, clean, or tend to young children back then. Few do now. I was an adult before I'd seen a man wash a dish in either grandmother's kitchen.

At some point in my early teens—not coincidentally, around the time the Spice Girls broke onto the world stage and feminism took on teenybopper form—I made an inner vow to not grow up to be a woman who cared about "those kinds of things." I would be different, I decided. A woman without walls.

I was twenty-one when I met Eric. He had come with mutual friends to the house I shared with eight roommates, and to this day he swears he fell in love at first sight. I was pulling a sweet potato out of the microwave as my dinner, almost triumphant in my lack of domestic prowess before this handsome stranger. *I'm not like the other girls, see? Love it or don't; love me or don't; but I'll never be your maid.* Happily, he wasn't looking for one.

During our engagement we took turns with another couple hosting dinner for each other. On their nights, Robbie and Danielle prepared elegant meals with herbs and sauces. On our nights, we made assembly-line mini pizzas out of Pillsbury biscuit dough and the kind of pepperoni you buy in the aisle instead of at the deli counter. Eric wasn't a cook and never expected me to be one either. We all laughed and ate and it was more or less pretty good.

But when we got married, something changed. Suddenly I *wanted* to cook, liked it even. I didn't have a particular knack for it, but with a decent recipe it usually didn't matter much. Cooking and other household chores became a rite of passage, ushering me into adulthood after all those loafing college years. I admired my ability to do this: to be a grown-up, to care for a five-hundred-square-foot apartment with attention and warmth. *Huh. Maybe this is the kind of woman I am after all. Maybe this is bringing me back to myself.*

I never enjoyed the cleaning chores as much and was happy to let Eric take the reins on scrubbing toilets, but I cooked near daily for years. I became vegetarian, then vegan, then back to vegetarian when I missed cheese too much. When we brought Alyosha home, motherhood made me even more curious about what this grown-up in me could do. I laundered cloth diapers every day with detergent I made from scratch and hung them on a line to dry. I made my own all-purpose cleaner. I fermented kombucha on our kitchen counter. I liked this life. I liked this me.

But after a few years and with the birth of Moses, my interest in homemaking began to wane as the care of two children consumed my attention. When Taavi was born, I dreamed of outsourcing the chores so I would be freed to divide my time between writing and cuddling babies. By the time Oscar came along, the work of the home had garnered not just my annoyance but my resentment. These days I'm more resigned but not necessarily more motivated. Thea wouldn't know a cloth diaper if one bopped her over the head. The kids are surprised when they have clean laundry. Sometimes they cheer.

It's normal for women to experience a similar evolution. We may even poke fun at our old selves when we get together with others, laughing at how perfect we had wanted to be and how earnestly we had tried. *How funny that I thought children had to be wearing clean pajamas to sleep! How sincere I was about never resorting to a McDonald's drive-thru!* It's a bonding ritual for us—a way for strangers to become friends and friends to become a village.

Sometimes we do it to new moms, and it stings. *Oh, she's still pureeing her own baby food. Wink.* Or was that an eye roll? Hard to tell with this cynicism clouding my vision. I've been in groups, and maybe you have too, where a woman who happens to excel in homemaking downplays her gifts in order to fit in with those of us who complain about it. The ax cuts both ways. It's our self-consciousness, not our freedom, that keeps us from celebrating what another woman can do.

Women are not static creatures. We will go through many metamorphoses and wear many hats over the course of our lives. What if it's not about being "this" or "that" kind of woman, but about exploring the things that are helping us discover the woman we are on the road to becoming?

Ten years ago, the woman I was becoming was curious about the power of my hands to create a sense of place. Right now, the woman I am becoming is curious about the power of my hands to type words that make women more whole. Both are holy work. Both have served me and others well. What is there to judge in myself now? What is there to judge in another?

Rethinking the Domestic Realm

Each of us has a slightly different relationship to housework. Some of you split the labor evenly with your partner. Some of you are in arrangements where your spouse does more than you. Some of you are responsible for all the homemaking chores because you are a single parent; some because that is the agreement, spoken or unspoken, that you and your spouse came to years ago. Some of you are fine with your current arrangement; some of you are miserable. But we are all affected by the long, complicated history between women and domesticity, and if we want a healthy relationship to this work, we have to reckon with that history.

Much has been written of the Industrial Revolution of the 1760s–1840s resulting in "the cult of domesticity" that bound women to matters of the household so that men, whose world of opportunity was daily changing, for better or for worse, would have a safe and amenable home to which to return at night. While men began working outside of the family property, women were encouraged to see the home as their personal industry—a space of their very own to control and rule. Gender roles and division were nothing new at this time, but this was the birth of the perceived inferiority of "women's work."

In the first half of the twentieth century progress was made toward opportunity for women outside of homemaking, but a second wave of the cult of domesticity came roaring in with a vengeance before long. After women filled the workforce to keep the country afloat during World War II, they were promptly sent back to the kitchen once the war was over—or, at best, demoted to positions deemed more "suitable" for delicate females, despite having performed quite well at their original jobs. As the country sought to recover from the collective trauma of the Great Depression and two world wars, a woman's domesticity became the mark of upward mobility. And everyone wanted to be upwardly mobile.

In *The Way We Never Were: American Families and the Nostalgia Trap*, Stephanie Coontz presents research about how the largely fictitious 1950s family became the idealized model for every generation since, and how that has always been not only an impossible standard but also a categorically unhealthy one for our collective imagination.

Coontz relays how in 1959 Vice President Richard Nixon famously argued with Soviet leader Nikita Khrushchev that capitalism was superior to communism because of the domestic comforts "designed to make things easier for our women."[1] This was the boom of things like convenience foods and labor-saving appliances, and yet contrary to what men in power told themselves, the innovations failed to improve quality of life for the female sex. According to Coontz, the amount of time women spent doing housework and childcare actually increased in the 1950s.[2]

While prior generations of women had relied on the assistance of hired help or live-in family members, the so-called domestic comforts of the 1950s created both an illusion of less work and an assumption that women no longer needed outside help. Domestic work became devalued as something that required no skill or particular care; there was no dignity or honor in the public perception of household labor. It was so "easy," so "convenient," that surely women enjoyed it. Surely they could handle it alone.

Advertisers' surveys from the era reported that women were finding housework to be "a medium of expression for . . . [their]

femininity and individuality."[3] While this was surely true for some women, just as it is true for some today, one has to wonder how honestly surveys like these were answered in a time when women who struggled to embrace the role of homemaker were assigned a mental illness diagnosis and even institutionalized.[4]

These days the cult of domesticity has a new spin, one of mommy wars and Pinterest guilt and Joanna Gaines–style homesteading for the elite. We have every "convenience" under the sun but are drowning in expectations, comparison, and the pressure to do it all. In deeply religious environments, home-making is still dangerously intertwined with female worth and godly duty. Even those who enjoy homemaking can feel con-fused by the onslaught of messaging. Those who don't enjoy it are ready to light a match.

Don't get me wrong, I am not one to eschew a perfectly good dishwasher. I love my Healthy Choice freezer meals. I am not trying to paint an overly romantic picture of the hardships of the past here. I know my grandparents used an outhouse, and I cannot emphasize enough how very much I do not want to return to that in the middle of a Midwestern winter. But I do think we suffered a terrible loss in our relationship with do-mestic work in the social shift of the last century. In our quest to make homemaking easier, we robbed it of its dignity by marketing it as work that can be done quickly, absentmindedly, and carelessly rather than work that requires care, attention, time, and love.

Saint Teresa of Calcutta (aka Mother Teresa) is credited as having said, "Wash the plate not because it is dirty nor because you are told to wash it, but because you love the person who will use it next."[5] This, I think, is what homemaking is all about: love for the people with whom we share a sense of place, love for ourselves and the commitment to practicing it, and love for the world of wonder that surrounds us. Is it possible to love a plate if God is in all things? A plate represents nourishment, it is community, it is provision, it is delight: these are divine marvels. I can find God in a plate. It is possible to love a plate.

We see these things when we choose to live with eyes wide open. We see that the plate is sacred, the plate is a symbol, the plate is worthy of care. Even the most mundane household chore has the potential to invite us into surprising places of contemplation if the work is held with mindfulness. But we are mothers; how many plates do we wash in a single day? I shudder to even estimate. Will we have a mystical experience after every breakfast? Sadly, no.

I don't expect to be enraptured into divine ecstasy while I pick up Legos. Homemaking is often an act of the will and not always something that lends itself to deep meditative prayer. We are not living in a monastery here, and the mere fact that we want a chore to feel spiritual does not automatically make it so.

But every once in a while, when the house is quiet and the sunlight from the window hits the stack of dish towels just right, we can see it: the rhythm of this life that we could never have earned, the safety and care that pulse through the rooms, the magic of having a corner of the world in which we fully belong. It is in these moments that our labor becomes prayer, whether or not we realize we are praying.

The Zen of Daily Life

Our house is a hundred years old, and she feels it in all her creaky, cranky joints. Even when she's clean she doesn't look very clean. Something is always breaking; something is always calling for attention. On top of the cooking, cleaning, and clothes washing required of living anywhere, our house seems to delight in coming up with new ways to put us to work. Sometimes we fantasize about moving someplace new, someplace built within our lifetime, someplace with white baseboards and a bathroom cabinet that is intact in the wall. We tire of the neverending litany of need.

By grace alone, our house is situated right across the street from the home of Iowa Artist Fellow Catherine Reinhart, who has become a dear friend to me as we journey together as creatives and mothers. Catherine came into my life at a time when I felt suffocated by the labors of homemaking. She too had experienced the ambivalence of adoring her children and dreading the work of keeping house; yet, instead of growing bitter as I had, she'd channeled her inner conflict into exploration through her fiber and textile art. Instead of giving way to resentment, Catherine had chosen the path of curiosity.

Catherine's art honors the rituals of caregiving: stacking, sorting, washing, pilling, braiding, mapping, mending. She points out that these repetitive acts are what provide comfort, ease suffering, and give us a sense of connection to one another. In her artist bio, Catherine explains, "As artist and mother, I am both archivist and field hand, creating studies in the accretion of domestic life and cataloging its labors. I disassemble, reconfigure, and alter abandoned textiles. Stratums of fiber in my sculptures reference sedimentary layers and the state of my laundry pile. I map the territory of my home-place with the visual language of topographic maps. With these works, I join the growing ranks of a constellation of new artist-mothers giving voice to the maternal and domestic experience."[6]

Befriending Catherine revolutionized homemaking as a spiritual practice for me. Not that I relish it now—to be clear, I don't—but the invitation to experience it as something rich in symbol has redeemed household labor from feeling entirely oppressive and burdensome. Where once all I could see was the cult of domesticity, I can now sometimes see the greater rhythm of humanity. On my very best days, I can envision housework as a subversive act of care in a culture that wants to rid itself of all that is inconvenient and dull.

In her book *Liturgy of the Ordinary*, Anglican priest Tish Harrison Warren writes, "I need rituals that encourage me to embrace what is repetitive, ancient, and quiet. But what I crave is novelty and stimulation."[7] Warren recalls one particular Lent when she decided to take up a new spiritual practice. Concerned that her habit of checking email and social media on waking up indicated an addiction, Warren set a Lenten intention to instead make her bed first thing every morning and then sit on it in prayerful silence. As the days went by, she began to notice that her need for instant gratification decreased and her capacity for spiritual awareness sharpened. The ritual of smoothing wrinkles and tucking in corners evoked contemplation of the Creator God who brought order out of chaos. The tangible practice of repetition and physicality elevated her soul to a higher awareness of Presence.

Like a growing number of Catholic, Episcopalian, and Orthodox children, several of my own kids participate in Catechesis of the Good Shepherd (CGS) as their formal means of faith formation. This Montessori-based approach to religious education is centered on the belief that the Spirit of God is already present and active in the souls of young children, and that what children need is not a religious prescription but a safe space to discover God's movements within them in a dignified way. The adults provide the setting, structure, and a vast selection of age appropriate "work." But it is the children's job, from as early as three years old, to follow their curiosity, trust their inner promptings, and explore ritual and Presence through their work (what we normally call play).

What has struck me most through the years of our family's participation in CGS is the way this approach uniquely equips children to encounter the divine in their daily lives. Instead of coming to church to learn things about God from a teacher, my children come to church to discover how God dwells within them through everyday actions. One of my sons is drawn to repetitive tasks like poking holes around the outline of crosses, card after card. Another wants to set up the chalice and paten, his tiny chest puffing with importance at being entrusted with the things of the altar. The mood in the atrium is quiet and reverent. The children know that this is their sacred space, their sacred work, and they conduct themselves accordingly. At CGS I witness my kids fold, polish, sort, and prepare—the same actions I spend so much of my time doing at home, unmoved by the holiness of my own labor.

It's interesting how the rhythms of religious ritual mirror the rhythms of homemaking. Watching my son gingerly pour dry beans into a jar reminds me of watching our priest pour the elements of the Sacrament. In the liturgy of the Mass we rise and kneel, we recite and repeat, we eat and drink. After we ingest the Bread of Life, the priest tidies up the altar like I do my own kitchen: wiping down the chalice, neatly folding the linens, balancing it all on a tray to be carried off by another for a proper cleaning. In the repetition there is comfort and knowing. In the attention to detail there is a human story.

Every religious tradition has a liturgy in the technical sense of the word, even the charismatic ones that think they don't. A liturgy is just the order in which we do things: the habits that form our communities, the way we worship that which we love. All over the world, in thousands of different ways, the human heart reaches for the transcendent through order and repetition. This is especially true for the most ancient traditions, those that have stood the test of time. Our everyday routines are not sexy; there is no rush of endorphins, no instant gratification. But the simple, redundant acts of being human seem to be the truest form of worship we can muster.

A Celebration of Wear

A few years ago Eric and I splurged on a navy blue sectional couch, figuring we needed sufficient seating for at least seven on a daily basis. There was really only one way to situate such a monstrous piece of furniture in our living room, and one end sits directly under a window, where every single one of our five children (and the dog) insists on perching in order to survey the neighborhood like little watchmen on a wall. Unsurprisingly, that particular couch cushion quickly wore down under their weight and movement, and in a matter of months we had an enormous hole with stuffing that was always falling out.

I was annoyed. I knew I could do an amateur mending job, but I also knew it would never look like it once did. As I hunted down some navy thread in my little sewing kit to tend to the damage, a spool of bright teal thread caught my eye instead. Hmm.

The next week when my neighbor Catherine and her son came over, I showed her my unruly, mismatched mending job. "I decided if I had to mend it, and it was never going to look perfect anyway, I wanted to make it funky and cheerful," I said with a grin. She smiled back at me, eyes sparkling. "I love it," she said. "A celebration of wear."

A celebration of wear. Tending to that which is in our care—whether that be babies' bottoms, scalded pots, or ripped couch cushions—can remind us of the miracle that is being alive. It reminds us how lucky we are to be in relationship with others: to have a sense of belonging and place; to have a life so full, so rich, that material things get demolished because we and the people around us are sucking the marrow out of the bones of every day we are given.

This old, beat-up home is ours to mend, one task at a time. What if I saw it not as an inconvenience but as an honor? This house has cradled families for over a century, has seen deep anguish and great joys, has kept secrets and held celebrations. This home tells a long story, and I am only one small part of it, but today it is I who am charged with carrying the candle by mending cushions and cleaning windows. I have the privilege of devoting tender hands to this abode where so many before us carried on their lives. A sense of place connects me to them as well as to those who will come later and, by extension, to the entire human race. The work of the home is only burdensome if I see it that way.

This is about much more than dusting ceiling fans or steaming vegetables or scrubbing mildew. This is about a currency of care, a ritual of presence, a cultivation of belonging. The work of the home is not about a mythical feminine ideal that leads only to death; the work of the home is about living a fully awakened life.

—— Going Deeper ——

Practice incorporating domestic labor into your spirituality. Select one task that you can engage in with your whole heart and determine what time of day you're unlikely to be interrupted—perhaps during naptime if you're at home with little ones, or in the evening after the kids are in bed.

Whether the chore you've chosen is scrubbing dishes, folding laundry, or sweeping floors, go slowly and allow yourself to become fully present to the repetition of the task while you work. You might select a short prayer or mantra to repeat aloud along the way, or you might choose one of the following questions to meditate on:

What does this action say about how I wish to engage in the world around me?

What does this action say about the nondisposable nature of both the earth and people?

What story does this tell about my life? About the human experience?

How does my soul benefit from acts of repetitive care?

thirteen

Living Incarnation

Finding God in Our Bodies, Home, and Earth

One thing that has surprised me most about parenting is how often you get hit in the face. In my experience, it's almost never on purpose—rarely have I had a pudgy little hand attempt to reprimand me for denying it sugar—but it's an occupational hazard of living alongside humans who have yet to figure out how their bodies affect other people. I've had little ones in the house for over a decade, and my nose has now met with the back of each of their heads multiple times. Flying toys have collided with my jaw. Wayward elbows have sent my teeth down on my own tongue.

I console myself by thinking this proves I am an engaged mother who is very often down on her children's level, but I think the argument could also be made that I am just slow to catch on to the fact that parenting preschoolers necessitates helmet usage. A few years ago I found myself in the office of an ophthalmologist who had just diagnosed a retinal detachment. His brow furrowed. "That's unusual. We ordinarily see this in the elderly or perhaps those who play contact sports." He unconsciously evaluated my soft mom bod, "Do you . . . play lacrosse?"

"No, but I have two toddlers, which is kind of the same thing," I quipped, to his befuddlement.

Two days later I went under anesthesia so the doctor could repair my retina and prevent me from going blind in my right eye at thirty-five years old. I was eighteen weeks pregnant at the time. Deep within the dark of my womb a baby girl danced and spun as surgeons salvaged what threatened to be lost.

Recovery was not painful but rather monotonous: I had to lie down on my right side all day, every day, for over a week. As I monitored eye drops and sanitation and understood better what it is to age and break, a child's being wove more intricate within me, her kicks keeping me company in the loneliest hours. My body bore witness to both its decay and generativity, captivating me with the story it told of life, death, and resurrection.

Inasmuch as we are dying, we are also creating. Inasmuch as old things are passing away, we are also being made new. We are less of who we were and so much more of who we will be. Yet one is not bad and the other good; all things have their place when we believe that all things serve our ultimate rebirth. This is the story our bodies tell: for whatever way we are decaying, we are generating too. God is all in all.

God Is in All Things

The Christian imagination of incarnation is one of the things I love about my faith. The word *incarnation* is most commonly used in reference to Jesus of Nazareth and the embodiment of God in human form, but it needn't end there. Saints like Francis and Clare of Assisi, and their followers today, remind us that a theology of incarnation can change not only how we see Jesus but also how we see the world.

I believe women are uniquely wired to understand incarnational theology; perhaps this is one reason why the early Jesus movement was built on the backbones of women. To truly believe that God is embedded in the human body, or in the earth and its creatures, or in St. Francis's "brother sun and sister moon," requires a lens of compassion and connection that is innate to femininity.

The idea that God really could inhabit *everything* threatens the patriarchy, which operates through hierarchy, exclusivity, and an imbalanced distribution of power. Notice I didn't say "threatens men," for a well-balanced manhood includes femininity and therefore disrupts the rigid suffocation of patriarchy, which we can clearly see in Jesus's life of inner freedom—and the price he paid for it.

Christian mystics understand incarnation, as Teresa of Ávila demonstrated when she wrote, "Christ has no body but yours, no hands, no feet on earth but yours."[1] The catchphrase of the Jesuits, "God in all things," communicates a similar message. The incarnation of God, not just in Jesus but in all people and created life, is deeply central to the Christian message. Yet even those of us who assent to it in our heads fall short of believing it in our hearts, and nowhere is that more revealed than in our relationship with our own bodies.

When my retina detached, my initial response was not "What a marvelous opportunity to explore decay and generativity!" It was more along the lines of a few choice expletives and a bemoaning of "my stupid body." It pains me to even type those words, but that was indeed what came out of my mouth, and I've learned that the words we speak reveal our innermost beliefs.

When we speak of that bodily God-within-us-ness, it's far different than trite platitudes about self-love and body positivity. I'm not telling you to strip naked before a mirror and feel thrilled over everything you see (although if you do, I am cheering you on). I'm talking about going beneath our conceptions of "attractiveness" into a space where we are able to praise our bodies for being our physical connection to sacred experiences.

When I lead workshops on prayer, one of my foundational goals is to give attendees permission to engage with their bodies and senses. Sometimes there is hesitancy or resistance, whether spoken aloud or not. Sometimes people are already doing it but not acknowledging that's what they are doing. We in the Western world have believed the lie that our bodies have no business in the spiritual realm; we think our bodies are relevant only if the conversation is on purity or self-discipline (e.g., "I run every day because my body is God's temple").

It does harm to sever the different parts of ourselves; the more integrated we are, the more spiritual vitality, love, compassion, and joy we experience. The more we believe that the material world belongs to God, the more desire we will have to care for that world and the more tools we have for accessing the Spirit. Sometimes these tools are very practical: lighting a scented candle, creating art, doing yoga, breathing mindfully, gazing at icons, and listening to meditative chanting are all ways we can engage our bodies in prayer.

But incarnation is not a belief that can be taken up for half an hour and then put down again. To really incorporate a theology of incarnation into our spiritual lives, we are called to a greater sense of presence. Sitting in the grass for ten minutes, noticing the way the blades feel on your legs and the way the breeze moves through your hair, is a spiritual practice of equal value to any other. Whether or not you identify as a nature lover, your body *is of nature* and longs to reconnect with all that is enjoined to her. Reclining against a tree, standing over a body of water, or hiking local trails are all ways we can find grounding for our bodies and re-member them to our spiritualities. And the more we are able to experience our bodies as little incarnations that connect us to a larger story, the less inclined we are to critique, bemoan, or disassociate from them.

Considering What Is Sacred

There is untold power in embracing incarnation. Just as it bears potential to rewire how we find our being in our own bodies, it is equally potent to affect how we engage in our homes. Absorbing an incarnational worldview—one that says God is in all things and before all things and in whom "all things hold together" (Col. 1:17)—changes us. Most of us spend our lives with an image of God as a being who sits on a throne somewhere in the sky, far removed from the nitty-gritty of the human conundrum. The idea of an "out there" God permeates orthodoxy mightily. Many in the world, whether explicitly religious or not, labor under the idea of the divine being as a completely separate entity from themselves.

But what if the good news was a lot more, well, *good*? I believe it is. If the Spirit of God lives within all of creation—and it would be difficult to create a compelling argument otherwise—then that Spirit surrounds us, fills us, and mirrors itself to us always. Once you see it, there is no more unseeing; you will fall deeper and deeper into mystery, deeper and deeper into love.

At the end of your life, relatively few hours will have been spent in your place of worship or achieving impressive career accomplishments. The vast majority of the living that you do takes place within the walls of your home, with the people you most take for granted. If you are called to a life of incarnation, of bearing witness to the reality of a God who is fully present, then the minutiae of home life are what matter most.

To live incarnationally in our homes is to treat life as sacred. The way we speak, not just about our own bodies but to the souls under our roof, is sacred. Treating children with dignity and equality is sacred. Equitable division of household labor is sacred. Sex is sacred. Scrubbing toilets is sacred. Planting a garden is sacred. Catching wayward insects and moving them outside without killing them is sacred.

When I say sacred, I don't just mean that these everyday actions are worthy of our time and protection, but that they are an actual portal to the divine life. Sacred acts draw us further into God; further into mercy and justice; further into faith, hope, and love. The people and actions that make up our lives are seeds of divine encounter. If we treat them as seeds must be treated—with intentionality, care, and consistency—they will sprout, blossom, and bear fruit. And we will kneel on holy ground.

Wild Mercy author Mirabai Starr remembers what it's like to have young children. It's almost impossible to find adequate time for spiritual practices, she says; therefore, we need to be creative.

> Your family has to *be* your practice. . . . Women are learning to resacralize our ordinary embodied experience. We are no longer willing to wait for invitations from men's ancient elite clubs; we do not believe true spiritual experience is limited to these privileged spaces. Instead, we find the face of the Holy One in the faces of our babies and our lovers, our elders and our coworkers, the dirty dishes and the deep quiet that falls over our homes when everyone else is sleeping and we stand at the window, looking at the moon.[2]

Searching for the Sacred

When I think about encountering God in creation, I think of Alice Walker writing in *The Color Purple* that it "pisses God off" when you walk by the color purple in a field and don't notice it,[3] or Robin Wall Kimmerer asking permission from the land to pick a single strawberry in *Braiding Sweetgrass*.[4] People of color, particularly women of color, are often rooted in a bodily knowing about divine presence in the earth. I have found I need their teachings in my life.

Kaitlin Curtice, a Potawatomi woman who grew up disconnected from her tribal heritage and returned to it as an adult, has a valuable perspective on this. In her book *Native: Identity, Belonging, and Rediscovering God*, she writes:

> Growing up in the Baptist tradition, I heard little mention of communicating with God through the earth. On Sundays, we would often hear sermons about how prayer is something we should just *try harder at*, instead of something we enter into. . . . Now when I come to this park [to pray], I bring tobacco. I hear the trees speaking, and they remember everything. As the rocks invite me to sit, they're asking me to take a moment to remember. And when the water stills to reflect the blue Georgia sky, I am being asked to remember, to reclaim something.[5]

What would it look like for you and me to open ourselves to hearing the earth ask us to reclaim something? Could the trees really have a story to tell us about the work of the Holy One on this planet? Could mountains draw us deeper into divine presence? Could the animal life scampering around us breathe renewal into our souls if we stop to watch?

Most of us have probably had a revelatory moment in nature once or twice in our lives. Maybe we assume such things are rare flukes, an occasional happenstance to treasure but not to expect. But what if we *can* expect them? What if the lines between the material and the spiritual were never meant to be inflexible? If I told you that were you to step outside your door right now there would be a message from God for you, would you go? If you are the kind of woman to read this book in the first place, you probably would.

This is as true as true gets: the earth is alive with Spirit, and there is something for you every single day out that door. Maybe not lightning from heaven, but a movement of Spirit that speaks in that still, small voice inside you. The earth is inviting you to discover incarnation.

Protecting the Sacred

As I write this chapter, I do so on the property of Prairiewoods Franciscan Spirituality Center in Hiawatha, Iowa. The Franciscan nuns who sponsor the center are committed to ecospirituality. The little hermitage where I am staying is made of strawbale, with solar-powered electricity and radiant floor heating. I step outside my door and am enveloped in silence and wild Iowa prairie. I feel a part of my own soul healing through being physically present in a place where the land is held sacred. Soul and land always go hand in hand.

When human beings hold reverence for creation, when we collectively acknowledge that it too is incarnation, we treat it with the care it deserves. The mysterious cycle then funnels healing and spaciousness into our bodies and spirits. Today I let the trees fill me with their expansiveness. It was a gift.

But I know that when I return home in two days I will reenter my normal life that is, despite what I would wish, not very ecospiritual. Oh, I have excuses a mile long: we have five children, money is tight, life is hard, and we just need some things to be convenient. But can convictions really be called convictions if they aren't lived out? I'm wondering what my lifestyle reflects about my true belief system, what it reflects about my understanding of incarnation—or lack thereof.

Kenyan scholar and activist Wangari Maathai, the first Black woman to win a Nobel Peace Prize for her work in the Green Belt Movement, grieved the environmental degradation she saw resulting from her people's changing theology. Mount Kenya was once a holy mountain for the Kikuyu people, who believed that God dwelled on it and sent rain and clean drinking water from it. The people once treated the mountain with sacred reverence and took nothing that they did not need.

But well-meaning missionaries came and told the Kikuyu people that God did not live on Mount Kenya, God lived in heaven. Over time, reverence for the mountain diminished. If God did not live on the mountain, if it was not sacred after all, then humankind could do to it as they saw fit. Deforestation and crop encroachment began. The glaciers at the top began melting. Rivers began to dry up. Biodiversity became threatened. Maathai observes:

> We have been looking for heaven, but we have not found it. Men and women have gone to the moon and back and have not seen heaven. Heaven is not above us: it is right here, right now. So the Kikuyu people were not wrong when they said that God dwelled on the mountain, because if God is omnipresent, as theology tells us, then God is on Mount Kenya too. If believing that God is on Mount Kenya is what helps people conserve their mountain, I say that's okay. If people still believed this, they would not have allowed illegal logging or clear-cutting of the forests.[6]

This is a sobering and large-scale example of what happens when we disconnect our spirituality from the natural world. For all the hand-wringing over things like "taking God out of our public schools," where is the outcry over how we've taken God out of our mountains? Much of the environmental crises we currently face would be helped tremendously by a collective turn toward an incarnational faith.

Incarnational Work

One Easter morning, just like so many before it, I bent over a happily babbling baby to change his diaper. Holding him still with one hand while loosening a single baby wipe out of the tightly wound package with the other, I was mostly preoccupied with the litany of things to be done to get our family out the door in time for church. The stars would have to magically align for there to be any chance of making it on time. Of course, fate would hand me a diaper blowout.

As I wiped the feces from the cracks of my son's generous upper thighs, I was suddenly overwhelmed by the realization that *this is what the women were preparing to do on Easter morning*. Not changing diapers but changing burial clothes; not wielding rash cream but wielding spices and ointments for a decaying body. They were readying themselves for the work that has long been taken up by women: the dirty work, the earthy work, the incarnational work. The work that men were too busy or too proud to do.

Historically, women have known the sacredness of the physical, whether or not we have been able to articulate it. We are the ones who push eternal beings into the realm of time and space. We are the ones who tend to the bodies of those passing back to the other side. And every day in between, women care for the sanctity of earthly existence in all her forms and phases. A risen Christ could not have appeared first to anyone else: we are the gatekeepers of life and death. What a thing it is, to be a woman.

—— Going Deeper ——

Carve out time to spend in nature, free of agenda. It might be your own backyard for half an hour or it might be a weekend camping trip at a national park. The details are not as important as the simple fact that you do it and that you do it without placing demands on the outcome. I'm going to refrain from giving explicit instructions, but below are a few starting points in case you need some handrails. Feel free to either use or ignore them. This time is for you alone.

> *What is one element of nature that I feel drawn to today? An animal, tree, body of water, wind? Perhaps that drawing I feel is because it has something to say to me.*
>
> *How might God be answering a quandary in my life through this engagement with nature?*
>
> *What do I feel in my body?*
>
> *Practice active listening. Expect to be shown new ideas, thoughts, or realizations.*

fourteen

Reimagining God

Making Space for a Divine Motherhood

Women are largely denied the opportunity to see themselves in God's image.

It's not just a Christian problem; other major religions share the omission. If pressed, most of us would say that God is neither male nor female, but our speech, imagery, art, and metaphors all communicate otherwise. Within biblical Christianity the Father, Son, and Holy Spirit are all referenced as "he." Religious art, such as the work of Michelangelo in the Sistine Chapel, depicts God embodied as a white male, and such imagery has so trickled down into the cultural imagination that even cartoons about God are white, male, old, and bearded.

It's true that this language and imagery emerged from the masculine wording of the biblical canon. (Well, *most* of it. There is maternal imagery sprinkled throughout the Old and New Testaments that tends to be overlooked.) There is enough academic exegesis on the reasons for this to last a lifetime of study, but for our purposes I will simply point out that the canon was compiled in an age when women were subordinate to men as second-class citizens and experienced systemic oppression.[1] Men were the ones who chose the wording of our Bible and men were the ones who decided which works would be included in our canon. Sure, they were divinely inspired, but they could not see their own social blind spots. Women were excluded from the process.

This population could not yet dare to imagine God in the feminine as well as the masculine. It would have shown a tremendous lack of respect within the time and place they lived—a hard truth, to be sure, but one that we can understand within its context in history. However, that doesn't mean that all these years later our own spiritual imaginations have to be stuck there too. If God is neither male nor female, and yet we routinely image God as male, then logic only follows that it would also be permissible to image God as female.

This doesn't mean we actually believe that the Source of All Things has a gender. But we are finite humans and metaphor is often the only way we can make sense of that which is transcendent. Throughout history humankind has imaged the sacred in all sorts of ways; there's really no stopping our brains and souls from doing it. But if we understand that creative explosion as a gift from God to reveal God's self to us, rather than as a trap that might ensnare us and lead us astray, we will find our spiritual lives unleashed into greater love, awe, and mystery—and we will likely find the church looks a lot more like the Jesus it claims to follow.

Father God and Mother God

At age four, I sat in the living room as my dad led our weekly family devotional time. My older sister, Elise, and I began discussing the gender of God—a "boy," of course. My father kindly tried to explain that God is neither boy nor girl but spirit. Four-year-old me wasn't buying it. Amused by my certainty that God was a boy, my dad asked, "Well, Shan, how do you know?" Without missing a beat, I retorted, "Because! Have you ever heard of a girl named God?"

My dad still loves to tell that story, and I admit it's pretty cute. But it is also a story that carries a lot of grief for me. Even at such a young age I had internalized the maleness of God to be a sacred truth, one that implied that half the people on the planet had a connection to God that I never would, one that intrinsically separated me from my Life Source. I couldn't articulate at four years old how that felt; in fact, it would be three more decades before I would be able to do so. But finally, in my mid-thirties, after a small but not insignificant life crisis, God the Mother found me.

Now hear me out. A feminine imagery of God does not automatically have to be "mother." It can be many things: sister, midwife, leader, teacher, guide, companion, and so on. If motherhood is a triggering picture for a woman (or man) for any reason, I would encourage them to find the metaphor that feels right to their own soul. But since this is a book on motherhood after all, exploring God as Mother feels intuitive and right.

Julian of Norwich was one of my earliest guides on the journey toward the divine feminine. The fourteenth-century anchoress witnessed a maternal God, even a maternal Jesus, in a series of mystical visions she called "showings." She wrote an explanation of these showings in a book, which was the first English language book penned by a woman. In her writing, Julian fluidly entangles the genders of God, frequently pointing to *his motherhood* and the way *he birthed us* on the cross. If the anchoress had written of her showings today, many would call her a heretic or false prophet. Catholic Twitter would virtually stone her. How her writings emerged unscathed from the scrutiny of the Middle Ages is beyond me.

In one of the showings, she saw and recorded the following:

Even as rightly God is our Father, so is God rightly our Mother; and this he showed in all, and especially in these sweet words where he says: "I it am." That is to say:

I it am: the might and the goodness of the Fatherhood.
I it am: the wisdom of the Motherhood.
I it am: the light and the grace that is all blessed Love.
I it am: the Trinity.
I it am: the Unity.
I am the sovereign goodness of all manner of things.
I am that makes you to love.
I am that makes you to long.
I it am: the endless fulfilling of all true desires.[2]

The phrase "I it am" can trip you up. But try to put yourself into a mystical frame of mind and stay with it. When I read this passage, I am reminded of the limitlessness of the divine, the absolute improbability of confining the Holy One to a box of our making. Julian of Norwich bears testament that the Father and the Mother are the same entity—even the same entity as Love, or the goodness of all things. Her revelation was so paradigm shifting that instead of continuing to see God as a being that exists, she could begin to see God as existence itself.

Daring to reimagine God has this effect on us. Like Mary giving her fiat and finding her limited view of God blown open, we too are invited to give permission to the Spirit to shake up everything we thought we knew. Are we free to stay within our spiritual comfort zones? Sure. But worship becomes so much more poignant when we unleash the tether we've tied around our hearts, flying free into the expansive arms of the holy.

A Rightly Balanced Spirituality

I once witnessed a robin building her nest, bustling to and fro between a bush in front of me and a tree behind where I happened to be seated to pray. I became enamored with her total dedication to her work as she gathered leaves and twigs to piece together, bit by bit, to create a safe haven for her babies. *I too am building a nest*, I thought to myself, for it was a time when I was deconstructing and rebuilding my faith. But almost as soon as the thought came into my head, I realized the metaphor broke down; the bird was building not for herself, but for her young. She was making a safe and holy space for her children. She was doing what mothers do best.

Maybe I am not the one building the nest after all, I realized. Maybe my work is just to watch the leaves and the twigs be gathered, noticing that it's being done and that it's being done for *me*. She continued her work as I thought and prayed (how often are those the same thing)—soaring past me, sometimes to my right, sometimes directly over my head. Once I thought she might run right into me. I knew her nest was directly behind me, but I resisted the urge to look. *Best to let her have her secret*, I thought. Best to honor her desire to be unseen.

This is what a Mother God is like: working faithfully, unacknowledged and often unthanked, on behalf of the creation she loves. There is no demand for attention or praise, only an invitation to something safer, more nurturing, and more tender than we can currently imagine. A patriarchal God demands our respect; a matriarchal God requests our awareness.

A few years ago I participated in a small group at my parish committed to devoting ourselves to St. Ignatius's spiritual exercises over the course of nine months. Participants would do the daily exercises at home and then we would gather together once a week to share our experiences, guided by two spiritual directors. This was the same year I had become drawn to the divine feminine, so I vacillated from week to week between loving the exercises and loathing St. Ignatius's overly masculine metaphors for God. In short, it was a very healthy place for me: one that caused me to explore pushed buttons and ask hard questions even while learning and growing deeply.

While going through the readings one particular day, I came across an unobtrusive sentence about praising the God who constantly labors for me. Immediately I pictured a woman in childbirth, laboring to bring her child forth into the world. I could see her moaning softly on her hands and knees, rocking to a rhythm that only she knew. Focused and attuned, she was fully present to the work of bringing forth something from seemingly nothing. She was phenomenal.

I realized that a few years prior I would have read this sentence and pictured a male working on my behalf; I was struck by how differently my brain would have interpreted the words. I would have seen not one laboring as though bringing forth life but one laboring so as to repair the things I'd gotten wrong. Sure, I would understand the labor as undertaken with mercy and patience, but nonetheless the work would be done because I had fallen short in some way. A God who constantly labors for me? *Clearly I'm still not good enough.*

But now I read it differently.

Now the words conjured an image of a Mother God laboring for me, voluntarily stretching herself to bring me into being, knowing that of course I am not fully mature yet—I am a preborn infant. I am exactly where I am supposed to be, and where I am is deeply good. *I* am deeply good. Not a problem to be solved or a pathetic thing to be saved, but a deeply good being who is wholly and compassionately loved. This is a space of healing.

I don't claim to represent the experience of every person of faith, or even every Christian. But it seems to me that this revelation puts language to the experience of many of us. The feminine elements in God are an important balance to the masculine ones. If all we have known of the divine is God the Father, we are walking with a spiritual limp, yes, even those of us who were lucky enough to be raised to see "him" as loving and tender rather than aloof or stern.

The Chinese Taoist concept of yin and yang illustrates this well. Yin and yang are two halves that come together for wholeness, yin symbolizing the feminine and yang symbolizing the masculine. Every human being has both within us, and both are within the divine as well. When you split the two apart, it upsets the equilibrium of wholeness. Only when they are integrated are they complete. What a beautiful way of understanding God.

Much healing would come to our church and to our world if the crafters of religious spaces would recognize the importance of integrating the feminine aspects of God into the masculine. When we sever a part of God's self, we also sever a part of our own self, both individually and as a collective whole.

The masculinity of God is not the culprit here. Imaging God as male is valuable and good for our spiritual selves because it leads us to things like reverence, healthy self-discipline, protection of the vulnerable, a sense of right and wrong, and a desire for a virtuous life.[3] But left unbalanced, a belief in a God who is exclusively male can lead us down a road of legalism, perfectionism, fear, self-criticism, and a plaguing sense of unworthiness. Sadly, many of our religious experiences have been marked by such things.

On the other hand, when we integrate the divine feminine into our understanding of God, we find we have an easier time internalizing compassion, inclusivity, radical acceptance, justice for the outcast, and unconditional love. In my own life the divine feminine has offered me a maternal invitation to rest and be present. After a lifetime of assuming that striving and sacrifice would always be required for my spiritual growth, this was good news indeed.

Embracing the Divine Feminine

Opening our hearts and minds to the divine feminine is one thing, but it doesn't automatically change thousands of years of religious imagery crafted to uphold a focus on the divine masculine to the exclusion of all else. Most of us in the Western world will rarely, if ever, lay eyes on a visual rendering of God that is feminine unless we are ferociously seeking it out.

For this reason, visual depictions of Mary have served as a way for me to find my feminine experience represented in the sacred. I realize that the historical Mary of Nazareth was a human being like myself, but the veneration of her in my Catholic tradition has opened up a path for me to see a Mother God imaged back to me. The incredible vault of sacred art surrounding the Virgin Mary has become a holy part of the human tradition precisely because it speaks to something far bigger than Mary herself. The Marian archetype transports us beyond the young teen from Nazareth and into a space where we can begin to imagine the way a maternal God might gaze at us, the children of her affection.

When we admire Leonardo DaVinci's *The Madonna and Child*, for instance, with Mary breastfeeding baby Jesus, we might feel moved by their humanity, by the fact that they once engaged in the same daily acts of love and nurture that we do with our own children. They become relatable, knowable, and therefore more inspiring.

But something else happens too. Something deep within our soul stirs to life and recognizes this image as *other than*. Our inner senses touch the reality that we are beholding a visual representation of not just a historical mother and son but also of ourselves being cradled and nourished by a Heavenly Mother.

Similarly, dark-skinned Madonnas like Our Lady of Kibeho in Rwanda and Our Lady of Guadalupe in Mexico have been important mirrors for our sisters and brothers of color throughout the generations, proudly serving as reminders that the divine is not a Caucasian male. Representation matters, whether we're talking about ethnicity or gender or an intersection of the two.

Visual depictions of Mary in her many forms have touched the hearts of women and men all over the world and throughout history because we all, female and male, are unconsciously starved for assurance of a divine motherhood. What we feel stirred to worship is not Mary as an end in herself, but rather the Mother Who Creates and Sustains All.

Most Protestants I know are wary of Mary, choosing to overlook her or downplay her significance lest they toe the line of perceived idol worship that makes them so nervous about many of their Catholic neighbors. But what I have written in this chapter will be an uncomfortable blurring of lines even for many Catholics.

There is overlap here in what I said about fertility statues in chapter 9. When the feminine is crafted in a way that points our gaze toward the divine, it is never wrong to permit love from bursting forth in our hearts. These are just *things*, these paintings, icons, or statues: neither bad nor good but for how they are used. Do they drive us deeper into love for God or push us further away? That is the only measuring stick we are obligated to hold. It is a falsehood to insist that some things are sacred and some things are not—after all, "the earth is the LORD's, and everything in it" (Ps. 24:1).

Experiencing adoration and prayer when we behold renderings of the divine feminine does not constitute worshipping idols. If anything, the insistence on worshipping an exclusively male God is much more idolatrous. A god made entirely in man's own image, not worshipped in fullness but only for the parts that are convenient, comfortable, or retain power for those at the top? If anything is idolatry, it is that.

Clarissa Pinkola Estés explores the implications of a Mother God through the Marian archetype in her book *Untie the Strong Woman*. She writes,

> I have listened to some few theologians speak about Our Lady as though she is an appendage to a group of historical facts. Neither is she, as some charge, a superstition. She is not an obedient building made of cement, marble, or bricks. She is not to be used as a length of holy wire to bind us all to docility, severing the other thousands of traits given by Creator to us all for being beautifully and reasonably human and soulful. *Holy Mother is not meant to be a fence. Holy Mother is a gate.*[4]

My prayer for you, dear reader, is this: may Holy Mother be the pearly gate through which you walk into heaven right here on earth.

—— **Going Deeper** ——

Spend some time journaling about the inner movements you noticed within you while you read this chapter. Did you experience discomfort? Shock? Hope? Unease? Nurture? Empowerment? Explore those feelings.

Journal about the metaphors for the divine that you have internalized in your life so far and whether they have changed or remained the same. How has that representation of God shaped your personal spiritual experience? How has it formed the way you see yourself?

As you examine the diverse ways to imagine God, ask yourself these questions:

Which images of God do I feel called to hold on to?
Which do I feel called to release?
Which do I feel called to add?

Find one piece of art that ignites your heart to reimagine God as Mother. Purchase it, print it out, or create something yourself out of any medium you choose. Keep this visual reminder in your home and see how your relationship to it unfolds.

Benediction

May the daughter in you feel delighted in and protected, so that you may live as though you have nothing to lose. In belonging to yourself may you believe you can enflesh every dream that stirs your heart. May the purity of your fire be only kindled and never snuffed out.

May the mother in you make sacrifices without losing herself, so that when you extend nurture it is from the deepest chamber of love and not the snares of resentment. In birthing awe, life, and mystery, may you bring forth divine activity on the earth. May you offer arms of belonging to the vulnerable and the lonely, enveloping every living thing.

May the grandmother in you trust the inner wisdom you once doubted. In knowing yourself, may you come to know others more fully. In loving yourself, may you find you love others more freely. May you wink at sister death in all her forms, knowing nothing that is gone has really been lost.

And until all things once more find Oneness, may our Mother who art in heaven hold you in the palm of her hand.

Amen.

Acknowledgments

They say no man is an island, but perhaps it is women who understand this in an embodied, constant way. As I wrote this book, I was often moved—sometimes to tears—by how acutely I felt the presence of the many people who had shaped the woman I was becoming.

Thank you to my agent, Keely Boeving, who believed in this book from the beginning and has been a trusted adviser and advocate as I have fumbled my way into a career. The work of my editor, Katelyn Beaty, made this a better manuscript. Thank you for not allowing me to minimize myself.

Thank you to Paula Gibson and Rosanna Tasker, who created a lovely and inspiring cover that captures the spirit of this book. Thank you also to Erin Smith, Jeremy Wells, Julie Zahm, and the entire team at Brazos Press for enthusiastically receiving this project and bringing it to life and into women's hands.

These past few years of writing for Franciscan Media and for the Jesuits of Canada and the US have made me a better writer and a better Catholic. I am deeply grateful for your friendship and for the inclusive, impassioned Christianity you have represented to me.

During the months of book writing, as well as before and after, I have been buoyed by the wisdom and camaraderie of several dear writer-mother friends: Kayla, Lindsy, Laura, Cameron, and Stina. Erica Campbell, you have been my biggest cheerleader, and I would be a much lonelier me without you. Thank you also to my local mom friends in Ames, Iowa, and the dear Internet women whose friendships have nourished and nurtured me.

Thank you to the desert women of Soul Sanctuary 2019 for being beacons of divine light when my world and consciousness were turning upside down. I like it better this way. Thank you especially to Allison Weber for your devoted friendship. I never imagined someone who is not a mother loving this motherhood book the way you have, but that speaks to the expansiveness of your soul. I'm so glad Our Lady of Guadalupe brought us together.

The words and art of countless women of color have opened my eyes to the fact that all motherhoods are not created equal and that intersectionality is imperative to the conversation on feminism. I can write only my own story, never yours, but I promise to continue reading, witnessing, listening to, and paying for your stories with honor and deepest respect.

My spiritual director, Mary Jo Pfiefer-Wulf, has been a godsend in my life, and her fingerprints are all over this book. Thank you for patiently pointing me back to myself.

I am lucky to have Nell Donahoe for a grandmother; she knows a thing or two about being a working mom herself and yet always makes me feel like I'm doing something impressive. Thank you to my parents, Randall and Kay, for the hundreds of hours of childcare they provided so I could write this book and so that Eric and I could have room to breathe. I'm glad you chose to spend retirement near us. Thank you for moving close by.

Thanks to my sister, Elise, for hunkering down in a hotel room with me as I wrote this book proposal in the very beginning.

It's lucky we both like pizza and bathrobes. Thank you also to Prairiewoods Franciscan Spirituality Center in Hiawatha, Iowa, for being the perfect place to find the inner reservoir to finish this manuscript—a special shoutout to Grandmother Oak, a queen among trees.

My in-laws, Betty and Charles, are an incredible source of support from afar. Thank you for the unconditional love and the knowledge that you will always be there for us. Similarly, thank you to my brother, Kris, who always has my back when I need him.

Alyosha, Moses, Taavi, Oscar, and Thea: you are the lights of my life. You are worth every drop of blood, sweat, and tears that it takes to be your mama. I will never stop adoring you.

It takes a man of receptivity to walk with a woman who is on a journey of unpacking the effects of patriarchy and sexism. It is not always a pleasant adventure, as the footpath bears a lot of carnage. Eric Evans, thank you for being who you are—a true partner for me in every sense of the word. I love you.

Notes

Chapter 1: Forging Identity

1. Christena Cleveland, "'Self-sacrifice as the pathway to significance' is one of whitemalegod's most impressive deceptions," Facebook, May 29, 2020, https://www.facebook.com/drchristenacleveland/photos/a.443435289069330 /3037584676321032.

2. Sue Monk Kidd, *The Dance of the Dissident Daughter: A Woman's Journey from Christian Tradition to the Sacred Feminine*, 20th anniversary ed. (New York: HarperOne, 2016), 52–53 (emphasis in original).

Chapter 2: Maintaining Boundaries

1. Glennon Doyle, Twitter, January 2, 2017, https://twitter.com/glennon doyle/status/815952818561490944.

2. Celeste Ng, *Little Fires Everywhere* (New York: Penguin, 2017), 293.

3. Quoted in James Munson, "You're More of a Virgin Than You Think," *Yukon News*, August 11, 2010, https://www.yukon-news.com/business/youre -more-of-a-virgin-than-you-think/. The discussion in the article focuses on Hudson's book, *The Virgin's Promise: Writing Stories of Feminine Creative Spiritual and Sexual Awakening* (Studio City, CA: Michael Wiese Productions, 2009).

4. See Marilyn Frye, *Willful Virgin: Essays in Feminism* (Freedom, CA: Crossing Press, 1992).

5. Quoted in Munson, "You're More of a Virgin Than You Think."

6. Quoted in Munson, "You're More of a Virgin than You Think."

7. Brené Brown, "Boundaries," The Work of the People: Films for Discovery & Transformation, 2021, https://www.theworkofthepeople.com/boundaries.

Chapter 3: Holding Tension

1. "Oprah's 2020 Vision Tour Visionaries: Lady Gaga Interview," filmed January 4, 2020, in Fort Lauderdale, Florida, http://www.youtube.com/watch?v=f8iNYY7YV04.

2. For more on Ignatius's teachings, see Kevin O'Brien, SJ, *The Ignatian Adventure* (Chicago: Loyola Press, 2011).

Chapter 4: Reclaiming Solitude

1. Paris Lees, "From the Archive: Emma Watson on Being Happily 'Self-Partnered' at 30," *Vogue*, April 15, 2020, http://www.vogue.co.uk/news/article/emma-watson-on-fame-activism-little-women.

2. Joan Chittister, *Between the Dark and the Daylight: Embracing the Contradictions of Life* (New York: Image, 2015), 108.

3. As quoted in Terry Tempest Williams, *When Women Were Birds: Fifty-Four Variations on Voice* (New York: Sarah Crichton Books, 2013), 172.

Chapter 5: Following Anger

1. *Comedians in Cars Getting Coffee New 2018: Freshly Brewed*, episode 11, "Alec Baldwin: Gyrating, Naked Twister," created and produced by Jerry Seinfeld, original air date July 6, 2018, Netflix.

2. Soraya Chemaly, *Rage Becomes Her: The Power of Women's Anger* (New York: Atria Paperback, 2019), 100.

3. "Sexual Assault, Domestic Violence, Child Abuse Statistics," The Center for Family Justice, 2021, https://centerforfamilyjustice.org/community-education/statistics/.

4. Sarah Bessey and Jeff Chu, "Climbing the Mountain of Injustice with Austin Channing Brown," Evolving Faith (audio blog interview), https://evolvingfaith.com/all-podcast-episodes/episode-2.

5. Sue Monk Kidd, *The Dance of the Dissident Daughter: A Woman's Journey from Christian Tradition to the Sacred Feminine*, 20th anniversary ed. (New York: HarperOne, 2016), 218.

Chapter 6: Staying Curious

1. Brit Barron, *Worth It: Overcome Your Fears and Embrace the Life You Were Made For* (Minneapolis: Broadleaf Books, 2020), 25.

2. Beatrice Bruteau, *What We Can Learn from the East* (New York: Crossroad, 1995), 3.

3. Mirabai Starr, *Wild Mercy: Living the Fierce and Tender Wisdom of the Women Mystics* (Boulder, CO: Sounds True, 2019).

Chapter 7: Cultivating Patience

1. Brie Stoner, "God Interrupting," Center for Action and Contemplation, June 27, 2019, https://cac.org/god-interrupting-2019-06-27/ (emphasis in original).

2. Leni Dothan, "Motherhood: A Visual Contract," *Image* 102 (Fall 2019): 36.

3. Tom Shadyac, director, *Evan Almighty*, written by Steve Oedekirk (Hollywood: Universal Pictures, 2007).

4. Karen Maezen Miller, *Momma Zen: Walking the Crooked Path of Motherhood* (Boston: Trumpeter Books, 2007), 40–41.

5. Julian of Norwich, *Revelation of Love*, ed. and trans. John Skinner (New York: Doubleday, 1997), 26.

6. Robert Elmes, quoted in Jennifer Conlon, "Last Stop on the L Train: Detroit," *The New York Times*, July 10, 2015, https://www.nytimes.com/2015/07/12/fashion/last-stop-on-the-l-train-detroit.html.

Chapter 8: Heeding Intuition

1. David Yates, director, *Harry Potter and the Half Blood Prince* (Hollywood: Warner Bros., 2009).

2. Terry Tempest Williams, *When Women Were Birds: Fifty-Four Variations on Voice* (New York: Sarah Crichton Books, 2013), 124.

3. Joyce Rupp, *The Star in My Heart: Discovering Inner Wisdom* (Notre Dame, IN: Sorin Books, 2010), 85.

4. Laura Jean Truman, "Mary Consoles Eve: Two Voices," Dec. 11, 2017, https://laurajeantruman.com/2017/12/11/mary-consoles-eve-two-voices-advent/.

5. Lisa Sharon Harper, *The Very Good Gospel: How Everything Wrong Can Be Made Right* (Colorado Springs: Waterbrook, 2016).

6. Harper, *Very Good Gospel*, 87.

7. Austin Channing Brown, "Trouble the Narrative," Wild Holy & Free, May 30, 2020, https://austinchanning.substack.com/p/trouble-the-narrative.

8. Catechism of the Catholic Church (3.1.1.6), available at https://www.vatican.va/archive/ccc_css/archive/catechism/p3s1c1a6.htm.

9. Kathy Khang, *Raise Your Voice: Why We Stay Silent and How We Can Speak Up* (Downers Grove, IL: InterVarsity, 2018), 21.

Chapter 9: Embodying Hospitality

1. Clarissa Pinkola Estés, *Women Who Run with the Wolves: Myths and Stories of the Wild Woman Archetype* (New York: Ballentine Books, 1992).

2. One good source to consult on the celebration of menarche is Abigail Brenner, *Women's Rites of Passage: How to Embrace Change and Celebrate Life* (Lanham, MD: Rowman & Littlefield, 2007).

3. Brenner, *Women's Rites of Passage*, 20.

4. Christy Angelle Bauman, *Theology of the Womb: Knowing God through the Body of a Woman* (Eugene, OR: Cascade Books, 2019), 125.

5. Bauman, *Theology of the Womb*, 121.

6. Molly Caro May, *Body Full of Stars: Female Rage and My Passage into Motherhood* (Berkeley, CA: Counterpoint, 2019), 164–65.

7. May, *Body Full of Stars*, 164.

8. Robin Wall Kimmerer, *Braiding Sweetgrass: Indigenous Wisdom, Scientific Knowledge, and the Teachings of Plants* (Minneapolis: Milkweed Editions, 2013), 97.

9. Cynthia Bourgeault, *The Wisdom Jesus: Transforming Heart and Mind—a New Perspective on Christ and His Message* (Boston: New Seeds Books, 2008), 31–32.

Chapter 10: Becoming Gentle

1. "Trust-Based Relational Intervention®," Karyn Purvis Institute of Child Development, Texas Christian University, 2021, http://www.child.tcu.edu/about-us/tbri/#sthash.wO9XxfjW.dpbs.

2. Aundi Kolber, "3 Ways to Heal from Past Wounds and Be a Parent at the Same Time," Crosswalk.com, January 23, 2020, https://www.crosswalk.com/family/parenting/ways-to-heal-from-past-wounds-and-be-a-parent-at-the-same-time.html.

3. Joyce Rupp, *Boundless Compassion: Creating a Way of Life* (Notre Dame, IN: Sorin Books, 2018), 57.

4. Andrea Miller, "Pema Chödrön on 4 Keys to Waking Up," Lion's Roar, July 16, 2020, http://www.lionsroar.com/pema-chodron-on-4-keys-to-waking-up-march-2014/amp/.

Chapter 11: Releasing Control

1. Anne Truitt, *Daybook* (London: Simon & Schuster, 2013), 192.

2. Joel Zwick, director, *My Big Fat Greek Wedding*, written by Nia Vardolos (Hollywood: Warner Brothers, 2002).

3. "Young Women with High Emotional Intelligence More Likely to Be Manipulative," PsyPost, February 17, 2016, https://www.psypost.org/2016/02/young-women-with-high-emotional-intelligence-more-likely-to-be-manipulative-40990.

Chapter 12: Valuing Work

1. Stephanie Coontz, *The Way We Never Were: American Families and the Nostalgia Trap* (New York: Basic Books, 2016), 29.

2. Coontz, *The Way We Never Were*, 28.

3. Coontz, *The Way We Never Were*, 28.

4. Coontz, *The Way We Never Were*, 35.

5. See Tsh Oxenreider, "You Love the Person Who Will Use It Next," The Art of Simple (blog), https://theartofsimple.net/forthelove/.

6. Catherine Reinhart, "Artist Bio," http://www.catherinereinhart.com/about-1.

7. Tish Harrison Warren, *Liturgy of the Ordinary: Sacred Practices in Everyday Life* (Downers Grove, IL: InterVarsity, 2019), 33.

Chapter 13: Living Incarnation

1. Cited in "Christ for Others," Together at One Altar, 2021, https://www.togetheratonealtar.catholic.edu.au/live/christ-for-others/.

2. Mirabai Starr, *Wild Mercy: Living the Fierce and Tender Wisdom of the Women Mystics* (Boulder, CO: Sounds True, 2019), 123–24.

3. Alice Walker, *The Color Purple* (Orlando: Harcourt, 1982), 196.

4. Robin Wall Kimmerer, *Braiding Sweetgrass: Indigenous Wisdom, Scientific Knowledge, and the Teachings of Plants* (Minneapolis: Milkweed Editions, 2013), 26.

5. Kaitlin B. Curtice, *Native: Identity, Belonging, and Rediscovering God* (Grand Rapids: Brazos, 2020), 71, 73.

6. Wangari Maathai, "The Cracked Mirror," *Resurgence and Ecologist* 227 (November/December 2004), accessible at https://www.greenbeltmovement.org/wangari-maathai/key-speeches-and-articles/the-cracked-mirror.

Chapter 14: Reimagining God

1. For theological explorations of this topic, consult Elisabeth Schüssler Fiorenza, *In Memory of Her* (New York: Crossroad, 1986); Elizabeth A. Johnson, *She Who Is* (New York: Crossroad, 1992); and Delores S. Williams, *Sisters in the Wilderness* (Maryknoll, NY: Orbis, 1993). For a less academic and more narrative style, I recommend Sue Monk Kidd's *Dance of the Dissident Daughter* (San Francisco: HarperOne, 2016).

2. Julian of Norwich, *Revelation of Love*, ed. and trans. John Skinner (London: Strathmore Publishing Services, 1996), 131–32.

3. Please note that these are not qualities exclusive to men or to women but rather archetypal qualities that rise to the surface when we look to the Divine as masculine or feminine. For further reading, see Clarissa Pinkola Estés, *Untie the Strong Woman: Blessed Mother's Immaculate Love for the Wild Soul* (Boulder, CO: Sounds True, 2013); Richard Rohr, *Eager to Love: The Alternative Way of Frances of Assisi* (Cincinnati: Franciscan Media, 2014); and Kidd, *Dance of the Dissident Daughter*.

4. Estés, *Untie the Strong Woman*, 19.

Shannon K. Evans is a writer with a Catholic spirituality and an interfaith heart. She is the author of *Embracing Weakness: The Unlikely Secret to Changing the World* and has written for Franciscan Media, Jesuits.org, *Geez*, *Relevant*, *America*, (in)courage, and *Verily*. She lives with her partner Eric and their five children in central Iowa. Learn more at shannonkevans.com or follow her on Instagram at @shannonkevans.